THE ILLUSTRATED ATLAS OF THE NINETEENTH CENTURY WORLD

THE ILLUSTRATED ATLAS OF THE NINETEENTH CENTURY WORLD

EDITED BY MONTGOMERY MARTIN

INTRODUCTION BY JONATHAN POTTER

STUDIO EDITIONS
LONDON

THE
Illustrated
ATLAS,

AND

MODERN HISTORY OF THE WORLD

Geographical, Political, Commercial & Statistical,

EDITED BY

R. Montgomery Martin, Esq.
Author of the "History of the British Colonies," &c. &c.

Previously published in 1851 as *The Illustrated Atlas and Modern History of the World* by
John Tallis & Company, London and New York

This edition published 1989 by Studio Editions Ltd.
Princess House, 50 Eastcastle Street
London W1N 7AP, England

Reprinted 1990

ISBN 1 85170 264 4

Printed and bound in Hong Kong

Publisher's Note

Although the text accompanying each illustration and map in the present edition represents a considerably abridged version of the original, every effort has been made to preserve the major points of content and the stylistic idiosyncracies of the nineteenth-century editor. We would also point out that, by the same token, the text reflects the original editor's viewpoints.

All the illustrations and maps from the original are included here, newly coloured for this edition.

Contents

Introduction

Moving, as we are now, towards the end of the twentieth century the reader enjoys an existence in which the availability and use of the printed word is often taken for granted. Despite the advent of computerization in the workplace, sometimes in the home, and in the mechanics of publishing, the dependence on printed matter - newspapers, books, maps, and instruction manuals is essential. In the mid nineteenth century literacy and the consequent availability of printed matter was not regarded as the common-place part of everyday life it is now.

The nineteenth century was a period of dramatic awakening and new understanding of the world - a second renaissance, the industrial revolution, increase in literacy, and a reassessment of moral and social responsibilities saw huge improvements in public knowledge and increased understanding of the world outside one's own native country.

Against this background of cultural expansion John Tallis' atlas of maps of all parts of the world may be seen as a vivid relection of the mid nineteenth-century world, not only with respect to geographical knowledge of coastal outlines, river courses and town locations, but also in the use of vignette views within the map's design showing the natives, occupations and appearance of different countries and regions of the world. In using these views and scenes Tallis' maps, based on recent accurate map-making, harked back to a tradition commenced in the seventeenth century by the Dutch map-makers of Amsterdam whose 'cartes à figures' and decorated double hemisphere maps are so well known and sought after by map collectors today. These Dutch maps, like those of Tallis two hundred years later, expressed far more than pure cartographic detail.

Relatively little is known about the background of the Tallis family or of their business history. However, the success of the business was such that theirs was amongst the first to publish atlases from both the British Isles and the United States, and the popularity of the maps is such today that the value of some individual maps is well over £100 each - the complete atlas bringing almost £2,000 in the auction rooms. Frequently referred to as 'the decorative series of world maps', these are attractively designed, informative pieces which combine the best elements of scientific cartography and decorative art as the great early map-makers did. The decorative borders and attractive vignette scenes contrasted vividly with the austere approach of many other comparable atlas publishers of the time, whose use of decoration was negligible although the cartographic quality of their output was undoubted.

John Tallis

The fact that father and son Tallis were both named John has given rise to some confusion regarding the development of the business. However, it appears likely that the more ambitious of the two was the son. Father had died in 1842, by which time their first major and now very rare publication had been issued. From 1838 a series of 'London Street Views' was issued. In pamphlet form advertisements on, and inside, the wrappers enclosed an oblong sheet on which was engraved a street plan with each building to be seen and business to be found illustrated in profile along the street in question. A view of a major landmark and a general map completed the engraving. This complex commercial venture provides students today with one of the finest records of London topography and business reference of the early Victorian era.

This attention to detail and quality of production, allied with the business sense of selling the advertising on the publication as opposed to retailing at a price based on production costs, were to stand the Tallis firm on a sound financial footing so that, within thirty years of the first record of Tallis as a bookseller in London, John Tallis & Co. was trading from addresses in London, Edinburgh, Dublin and New York.

At the time when Tallis' business was at its height, a further indication of the firm's success can be seen in a footnote to an illustration in *Tallis's Illustrated London* – a book of views of the metropolis. With reference to the illustration of Highbury Barn Tavern, Tallis remarks 'in this attractive place of resort, Messrs. John Tallis & Co., the publishers of this work, give their annual banquet and festival during the Whitsuntide holidays, to the persons in their employment, numbering upwards of two hundred'.

Unfortunately, John Tallis' ambition and imaginative schemes were to prove his undoing and, despite the success of his publications in the early 1850's, a business partnership formed in early 1854 in the name of London Printing & Publishing Company, was to lead to bankruptcy and disaster.

However, during the 1840's, Tallis had published, not only the series of 'London Street Views' but a number of other topographical works including Thomas Dygdale's *Curiosities of Great Britain* and the Reverand James Barclay's *The Universal English Dictionary,* and, by the end of the decade, John, with his brother Frederick who was also involved in the business, was developing the series of maps for which he is now best know. As with the London views the maps, of all parts of the world, were first issued as 'part-works' – weekly, or monthly instalments priced at '1s (one shilling) or 25 cents' whose staggered publications eased both the publisher's and purchaser's financial loads. At a time when book purchasing was a comparatively minority activity the publisher could encourage many more members of the public to subscribe using such terms.

The *Illustrated Atlas* had maps drawn and engraved by John Rapkin with the vignette views drawn and engraved by a number of prominent artists-cum-book illustrators. Issued as a complete volume from 1851, the accompanying text was written by Montgomery Martin, whose later work on the British Colonies used many of the Tallis maps. During the relatively short life of the publication of the atlas (until about 1865), constant revision of many of the steel plates was made. Five different editions of some of the Australian maps, for instance, are recorded – evidence of the rapidly expanding knowledge of that continent. Alterations were made not only to geographical detail, but also in the addition or deletion of some of the vignette scenes. The maps issued as part-works prior to 1850, in *The Illustrated Atlas* and in Martin's *British Colonies* from 1854, ended their printed life, without any vignette scenes, in geographical dictionaries and encyclopaedias about 1880.

Some later editions of *The Illustrated Atlas* incorporated a number of town plans, equally finely designed and engraved as the national maps. The selection of towns selected reflects their increasing importance within the industrial revolution, then in full swing. Plans which may be found are of: Bath; Bradford; Brighton; Clifton and Bristol; Exeter; Leeds; London and its environs; Liverpool; Mancheste and its environs; Newcastle upon Tyne; Plymouth and Devonport; Preston; Sheffield; Southampton; York; in Scotland – Aberdeen, Edinburgh, Glasgow and Perth; in Ireland – Belfast, Cork and Dublin; and abroad – Brussels, Boston and New York. Additionallya map of 'The Lakes of Cumberland, Westmoreland' and one of the railways of Great Britain may be found.

Map Printing Techniques

The techniques of printing had, over the four centuries since the earliest European printing, evolved, slowly at first, from individual hand printing methods to rapidly improving machine processes by the mid nineteenth century.

Tallis' maps were engraved on steel plates – a medium which replaced copperplate in the first quarter of the century – and which, through the metal's greater hardiness, lasted for a longer period of use, allowing for more 'impressions' to be taken of the engraving and for a more delicate, finer line to be engraved. On each metal the procedure was the same, in that the design would be engraved, or etched, in reverse on the flat sheet of metal, which would then be inked – leaving ink only in the etched line, any surplus having been wiped off – and finally have the paper pressed very firmly onto it in order to leave the printed line.

The very earliest maps had been cut on woodblocks, a process whereby the design would stand up from the woodblock 'in relief' which would then be inked and printed onto paper. This process is know as 'intaglio' printing as opposed to 'engraved'. The woodblock process had been in use until about 1540 when copper plates were found to be better to work with for fineness of detail and length of use. However, by the time Tallis was publishing, harder woods had become available from the tropics and woodcut illustrations were commonly found again in books and newspapers, the most widely available examples now being those from the *Illustrated London News*.

THE MAPS

Tallis' maps in providing a detailed view of the world accompanied by attractive vignette scenes also embody many fascinating aspects of a period of great social upheaval in the wake of the Industrial Revolution in Europe and, in the rest of the world, the opening up and development of each continent. A very brief examination of just a handful of the maps gives an indication of the exciting world which was becoming visible, and accessible to European eyes.

Obviously those maps showing the best known parts of the world are those of the European countries and, in these instances, the illustrations reflect an urban, more cultural existence than is seen on those maps of further flung parts of the earth. Thus the British isles map has detailed views of the major cities of London, Edinburgh and Dublin, and the map of England and Wales, which shows the development of the railways, has views of London (the Capital), Portsmouth (the most important naval establishment), Oxford (an ancient centre of learning), Newcastle (a thriving north coast industrial port), and Sunderland Bridge, one of the great iron bridges of the early nineteenth century. Further views, of the grandstand at the Race Ground Doncaster pay tribute to the building itself and to the 'genteel' pastime of horse racing, and a foxhunting scene completes this map as a compendious picture of life in England.

On mainland Europe the map of Germany shows scenes of Coburg, Cologne, Dresden, the Palace at Saxe Gotha, Luther's House at Frankfurt on Maine and silver mines in the Harz Mountains. Tribute is paid to the inventors of printing with the portraits of Gutenburg, Fust and Schoeffer.

Further afield, there are fascinating maps of parts of Asia including one of an area rarely mapped individually, that of 'Thibet, Mongolia and Mandchouria'. This is illustrated with vignette views of places rarely seen before by Europeans and a portrait of a Mongol Noble.

One of the best known areas of Asia, particularly to the British, who had surveyed the subcontinent during the 1770's and 80's, was India. Two maps show North and South India and a further map of 'British India' reflects imperial interest. A note in the book's text explains thus: 'In a previous number (of the part work) there were given two maps – one of Northern, the other of Southern India, but the magnitude and importance of this portion of the British Empire requires a single map, showing the entire peninsula of Hindoostan in one view.'

Less than eighty years before the publication of the atlas the continent of Australia was, to all intents, unknown. Western and Northern coastlines were known to navigators but the land was seen as inhospitable and, not until Captain James Cook's voyages of the 1770's, was the East coast known. Tallis' maps of Australia and its regions show how much development occured in a relatively short period. Illustrations of kangaroos, parrots, cockatoos, Aborigines, and of sheep farming provide a clear indication of the nature of the country, while the number of settlements, although each is small, testifies to the rapid colonization of the areas along the coast and river courses.

The maps of the New World provide an equally vivid picture of the ancient civilizations of north, central and south America and some of the animals and birds to be found there. European interest in the natural wealth of Latin America is seen in one vignette on the map of North America where the militia can be seen escorting a convoy of diamond workers and, on the map of 'Mexico, Californian and Texas' where a prospector is shown panning for gold, where the gold mining regions of California are marked on the map and the following reference appears in the text: 'To what extent gold may be found it is impossible to say, the whole of the mountains on the west coast of America probably abound with it.'

The map of North America has further interesting features. The projection chosen to show the map incorporates much of the North Atlantic; accordingly there are illustrations of Mount Hekla (Iceland's famous volcano), Eskimos with a dog sledge, and, surprisingly Cossacks. Normally associated with Russian Central Asia their presence on this map is explained by the fact that the area of Alaska did not belong to the United States until 1867 – prior to which it was, from the end of the previous century, part of the Russian Empire.

This brief examination of a few of Tallis' maps will hopefully encourage the reader to look further, for in these maps and their charming illustrations is a wealth of information reflecting the development from an unknown world to that which is so familiar today.

Jonathan Potter
December 1988

The Illustrations and Maps

A COMPARATIVE VIEW OF
THE PRINCIPAL
WATERFALLS, ISLANDS, LAKES, RIVERS
AND
MOUNTAINS,
IN
THE WESTERN HEMISPHERE.
MISSOURI. United States.
TRENTON. United States.
MONTMORENCY. United States.
CUYUHOGA. United States.
NIAGARA. United States.
BUTTERMILK. United States.
GUAYRA. Guayana.
ORONOCO. Colombia.
ST ANTHONY'S. United States.
OYAPOK. Guayana.
CATSKILL. United States.
WILBERFORCE. United States.
SILVER CASCADE. United States.
GENESE. United States.
RIO VINAGRE. Colombia.
TAQUENDAMA. Colombia.
NEW FOUNDLAND
NORTH I.
NEW ZEALAND
MIDDLE I.
S. Ysabel
CUBA
JAMAICA
VANCOUVER Id
Andros Id
Eleuthera
Bahama I.
Abaco
San Salvador
New Providence
Mariguana
St DOMINGO
C. Breton I.
PORTO RICO
Anguilla
Crab I.
Mansfield I.
Guadaloupe
Curacoa
Inague
Qn Charlotte I.
Albemarle
ICELAND
SOUTHAMPTON Id
Owhyhee
Dominica
Lawrence I.
NEW CALEDONIA
Martinique
South I.
S. Antonio
C. VERDE Is
S. Lucie
Kodiak
Akpatok I.
S. Vicente
S. Nicolao
Chiloe I.
S. Vincent
Falkland Is
Caviana I.
CUMBERLAND I.
S. Maria
Graciosa
Santiago
Grenada
AZORES Is
Anticosti
S. Jorge
Terceira
Charles I.
Tobago
Disco I.
Flores
Pico
S. Miguel
Georgia
Trinidad
Leech L.
L. Aylmer
L.S. John
L. Pepin
L. Silverio
Wollaston L.
Moosehead L.
GREAT SLAVE LAKE
LAKE ATHABASCA
L. Leon
Abbitibbe L.
Deer L.
L. NICARAGUA
L. WINNIPIGOOS
L. Nipissing
L. WINNIPEG
Cayman L.
L. MANITOBA
LAKE SUPERIOR
L. of the Woods
Doobaunt L.
Flatbow L.
L. TITICACA
L. Mistassinnie
LAKE HURON
LAKE MICHIGAN
L. MARACAYBO
Lesser Slave L.
L. Meshikeman
Great Salt L.
Clearwater L.
L. Simcoe
L. Champlain
L. Utah
LAKE ONTARIO
LAKE ERIE
GREAT BEAR LAKE
Temiscaming L.
Red L.
Chapala L.
L. Garry
Tule L.
MISSISSIPPI. MC KENZIE. ARKANSAS. ST LAWRENCE. R. DEL NORTE. RED RIV. COLUMBIA. NELSON. OHIO. COLORADO. POTOMAC. HUDSON. MAGDALENA. PARNAIBA. NEGRO. PILCOMAYO. COLORADO. URUGUAY. S. FRANCISCO. ORINOCO. PARA. MADEIRA. LA PLATA. AMAZON.
New Orleans
Ft Good Hope
Lit Rock
Quebec
Laredo
Natchitoches
Ft Vancouver
Ft Okenagan
L. Winnipeg
York Fact.
Cincinnati
Washington
Grand L.
Youth
NEW YORK
S. Cruz
Teneriffe
El Carmen
Neyn
Cayza
Calera
Penedo
Para
S. Tome or Angostura
Borba
Colonia
Buenos Ayres
Montreal
Ft Alexander
L. of the Woods
L. Nahuelhuapi
L. Bevedero
Joazeiro
St Fe
Obydos
Ft Simpson
L. Ontario
Santa Fe
L. Guanacache
Falls of Madeira
Ft St Louis
Slave L.
L. Erie
Caritipanos
S. Juan
Pto Salgado
L. S. Anna
Assumpcion
L. Athabasca
L. Huron
The Condor
Perpetual Snow
Highest point reached by Humboldt
Esmeralda
Loretta
L. Superior
L. Michigan
Sabara
Sta Cruz de la Sierra
Blocks House
L. Ipawa
L. Ober
Mississippi
Missouri
Ft Mandan
Potosi
L. Titicaca
Oropesa
Sette Lagoas
Quito
Riobomba
Punch Bowl
Mexico
Jeans
Big Horn
L. Biddle
Level of the Sea
1. Nevada de Sorata S. America
2. Illimani Do
3. Aconcagua Do
4. Chimborazo Do
5. Antisana Do
6. Cotopaxi Do
7. Arequipa Do
8. Descabecada S. America
9. Popocatepetl N. Do
10. Unniza S. Do
11. Citlalpetl N. Do
12. Tunguragua S. Do
13. Nevada de Merida Do
14. Browne N. Do
15. Cerro de Potosi S. America
16. Pichincha Do
17. Hooker N. Do
18. Nevada de Medici Do
19. Fremont Do
20. Mawna Roa Owhyhee
21. Coffre de Peroti N. America
22. Longs Peak N. America
23. Mt S. Elias Do
24. Mt Terror S. Victoria
25. Mt Erebus Do
26. James Peak N. America
27. Laramie Peak Do
28. Sierra de Cobre Cuba
29. Sierra de Grande S. Domingo
30. Mt Egmont N. Zealand
31. Mt Fairweather N. America
32. Duida Colombia
33. Bourbon Do
34. Blue Mts Jamaica
35. Mt Washington N. America
36. Black Mts N. America
37. Guadarrama S. Do
38. White M N. Do
39. Roan M Do
40. Blaaserk Greenland
41. Werner Do
42. Adams N. America
43. Jefferson N. America
44. Grandfather Do
45. Marcy Do
46. Madison Do
47. Monroe Do
48. Morne Garou S. Vincent
49. Souffriere Guadaloupe
50. Franklin N. America
51. Lafayette Do
52. Moose Hill Do
53. Jurullo Do
54. Pelee Martinique
55. Table Mt N. America
56. Camels Hump Do
57. Saddle Mt N. America
58. Mt Hekla Iceland
59. Catskill N. America
60. Kellington Pk Do
61. Gt Monadnock Do
62. Appalachian Pk Do
63. Wachusett Do
64. Kearsarge N. America
65. Cape Horn S. Do
66. Crowsnest N. Do
67. Anthonys Nose Do
68. Holyoke Do

Physical Geography of the Earth

Form and Motion

The earth is globular in form, and differs only from a perfect sphere by being slightly flattened at the poles. Its orbit round the sun is also somewhat elliptical, taking 365 days, 5 hours, 49 minutes and 57 seconds at the rate of 68,000 miles an hour. The equatorial circumference is 24,857 miles. The mean density of the whole earth is supposed to be five times greater than that of pure water. An imaginary line passing from north to south poles forms the axis on which the earth revolves, performing one entire revolution in 23 hours, 56 minutes and 4 seconds.

Divisions

The southern and northern hemispheres are separated by an imaginary line, the equator, which encircles the earth equidistant from both poles. The equator is divided into 360 parts or degrees, by which the longitude of any place is reckoned east or west of London. The distance of any place from the equator is called its latitude. The seasons in which the sun apparently moves on the equator are named equinoxes, while those in which it is at its greatest decline are called solstices. From pole to pole the earth is divided into five zones: the torrid zone lying between the Tropics of Cancer and Capricorn; the temperate zones on which the rays of the sun fall more obliquely; and the frigid zones within the polar circles.

Geology

As far as has been ascertained the formation of the earth followed the successive stages described in the Old Testament. It probably began as a dark, heated mass, which was cooled by the creation of an atmosphere and reduced to globular form by its motion round the sun. Evidence of this lies in the marked division of the earth into igneous (granite, basalt, lava) and aqueous (limestone, sandstone) formations of rocks. The earth's crust is supposed to be about 30 miles thick, the interior most probably being a fluid or gas hotter than anything we know.

Atmosphere

The atmosphere surrounding the earth is calculated to reach an average of 40 to 50 miles in height, and is composed of two substances: air and water in a state of vapour. Recent scientific experiments have determined that air contains 20.8 hundredths of oxygen and 79.2 of nitrogen, together with a few thousandth parts of carbonic and ammonial gases. Air is capable of expansion by heat and compression by cold, and its density decreases the further it rises above the level of the sea. The motions of air known as winds are caused by unequal distributions of temperature, and by the extent of ocean and elevation of the land. Within the tropics the general direction of the wind throughout the year is from the eastward, in the temperate zones from the westward. On the equator calms are prevalent, but towards the tropics there may be violent storms, termed hurricanes or typhoons.

Climate

Climate signifies the varieties of temperature and moisture in different countries, which depend materially on the degree to which they receive the rays of the sun; although local circumstances may cause great differences between countries in the same latitudes. Generally, islands and coast districts enjoy a more moderate climate than the interior of continents, because the ocean preserves a more equable temperature which it communicates to the adjacent country.

Designed & Engraved by John Rapkin.

Climate

Climate signifies the varieties of temperature and moisture in different countries, which depend materially on the degree to which they receive the rays of the sun; although local circumstances may cause great differences between countries in the same latitudes. Generally, islands and coast districts enjoy a more moderate climate than the interior of continents, because the ocean preserves a more equable temperature which it communicates to the adjacent country.

The Ocean

The seas which constitute about three-quarters of the surface of the earth are of various depths, the average being about three miles. Their profundity is probably equal to the height of land above their surface, that is about five miles at most. The average saltness of the oceans is about one twenty-eighth, and the chemical composition of sea-water varies little throughout the world. Tides, currents and winds keep the sea in a constant state of motion, although even the most violent storm does not agitate the waters lower than fifty feet below the surface. The tides are connected with the gravitational attraction of the moon.

The Land

About one fourth, or 50 million square miles, of the earth's surface is land, of which the largest portion is in the northern hemisphere. The most marked features of the earth are its lofty mountains, extensive lakes and vast rivers. The highest ranges are those of the Himalaya in India (up to 25,749 feet) and the Andes in South America (to 25,250 feet); the largest fresh-water lakes are in North America, where the rivers are also of great extent, the Missouri and Mississippi together being 3,500 miles long. The rivers of South America and Asia are also very long, the Yang-tze-kiang in China supposedly being the largest, and the Amazon flowing for 3,200 miles. Australia, which has been termed the 'fifth quarter' of the globe, is as yet imperfectly known. As the physical features of each country will be separately described, there is no necessity for giving further detail here.

Vegetable Kingdom

The plants of the world are almost numberless, 75,000 species being known to botanists. Those most generally diffused are the grasses, which are the most useful to man and the herbivorous animals. The vegetation of the torrid zone is remarkable for its variety and provides mankind with medicines, spices, cabinet woods, rice and sugar. In the temperate zones grain and edible roots abound. The ocean also contains numerous species of marine plants.

Animal Kingdom

Every portion of the earth, air and ocean teems with animated life, the greatest variety being found in the torrid zone. The known classified species can be divided into 330 mammalia, 2,600 birds' 400 amphibia, 1,000 fish, 800 insects,400 vermes.

Mankind

Cuvier has classed the great family of man under three heads: the Caucasian, Mongolian and Ethiopian. Anatomy and physiology confirm that despite the many varieties there is but a single genus, the differences in colour and cranial configuration being due to the effects of climate, soil, food and manner of living. The population of the globe is in round numbers 1,000 million, or 20 mouths to each square mile of the earths surface.

WORLD
ON
MERCATOR'S PROJECTION
ARCTIC OCEAN
NORTH PACIFIC OCEAN
SOUTH PACIFIC OCEAN
NORTH ATLANTIC OCEAN
SOUTH ATLANTIC OCEAN
INDIAN OCEAN
ANTARCTIC OCEAN
ASIA
EUROPE
AFRICA
AUSTRALIA
NORTH AMERICA
SOUTH AMERICA
RUSSIAN AMERICA
UNITED STATES
CHINESE EMPIRE
Mongolia
Tartary
Persia
Arabia
Tibet
Hindostan
Nubia
Abyssinia
Soudan
Desert of Sahara
Egypt
Greenland
Iceland
Spitzbergen
Lapland
Novaia Zemlia
Sea of Okhotsk
Bhering Sea
Bhering Str.
Aleutian Is.
Sea of Japan
Japan
Yellow Sea
China
Siam
Birmah
Bay of Bengal
Arabian Sea
Red Sea
Black Sea
Caspian Sea
Sumatra
Borneo
Java
Philippine Is.
Ladrone Is.
Caroline Is.
Marshall Is.
Sandwich Is.
Society Is.
Friendly Islands
New Hebrides
New Caledonia
New Zealand
Marquesas
Low Isles
Van Diemen's Land
Madagascar
Mauritius
Cape Colony
St. Helena
Ascension
Azores
Canary Is.
Cape Verde Is.
Falkland Is.
Tierra del Fuego
Cape Horn
South Shetland Is.
New Shetland
South Georgia
Gulf of Mexico
Caribbean Sea
Bahama Is.
Bermudas
Newfoundland
Nova Scotia
Hudson's Bay
Baffin's Bay
Melville I.
Parry Is.
Cockburn Isl.
Lancaster Sd.
Davis Str.
Arctic Circle
Tropic of Cancer
Equator
Tropic of Capricorn
Antarctic Circle
Enderby Land
Kemp Land
Adelie Land
Clarie Coast
Victoria
Perpendicular barrier of Ice
Kerguelen Land or Desolation I.
Prince Edward Is.
Emerald I.
Macquarie I.
Balleny Is.
VESUVIUS
THE PYRAMIDS OF GHIZEH
GIBRALTAR
LONDON
CONSTANTINOPLE
NIAGARA
PONT NEUF, PARIS
NOTE.
Steam Route to the Colonies Coloured thus
NOTE.
The British Colonies Coloured thus
E of G
W of G

The World On Mercator's Projection

Our knowledge of the geography of the earth has been acquired by great perseverance and industry, and even after the lapse of ages, there are many regions with which we are still very imperfectly acquainted. Sacred writ does not convey much information on the subject, yet the inspired writings of Moses, and that mysterious and beautiful record termed the Book of Job, contain various useful and interesting details, respecting parts of Asia and of Africa. The maritime knowledge possessed by the Phœnicians must have been extensive, but no records of it now remain. The Chinese, in the same age, were well informed respecting the coasts of Asia, but the Tartar conquests have caused either the destruction or the concealment of the written proofs of early civilization. The Egyptian knowledge was confined to the territories and shores adjacent to their own country. The expedition of the Argonauts to Colchis on the Euxine Sea, about 1280 or 1263 BC, formed a great epoch in maritime discovery. During the Homeric age, the earth was represented as an immense circular plain, surrounded on all sides by the *'river ocean',* above was the solid vault of the firmament, under which rolled the sun and the stars in chariots borne by the clouds. Beneath the earth was the vault of Tartarus, Hades or the caverns of the dead, and also the residence of the Titans, the enemies of the gods. The earth was supposed to be supported by pillars of which *Atlas* was the guardian. Thales (BC 540) taught the sphericity of the earth, and calculated with accuracy a solar eclipse. Herodotus (BC 445) travelled extensively in Europe, in Egypt, and in some parts of Asia. His writings laid the foundation of much geographical as well as historical knowledge. The Carthaginians were acquainted with the coasts of the Mediterranean, and the shores of Africa and of Europe, adjacent to the 'Pillars of Hercules' (Gibraltar). Alexander, by his conquests in the East, added considerably to a knowledge of Asia.

Eratoshthenes, keeper of the Alexandrian library was the first to introduce in maps parallels of latitude; he gave a rude sketch of Britain, but was ignorant of the existence of Ireland.

The distinguishing features of the different quarters of the globe have been given in the letter-press accompanying the maps of the eastern and western hemisphere. The lines on the annexed map show the steam routes of communication between several parts of the British Empire, which are coloured red. In a work of general reference, it is essentially necessary to state the geographical position of the principal places in the world, and I therefore give the following selection, chiefly on the authority of Mr. James Bell, who has evinced great research and persevering industry in his geographical labours. The longitudes are taken from the meridian of Greenwich.

THE WORLD
ON
MERCATORS PROJECTION
SHEWING THE VOYAGES OF
CAPTAIN COOK ROUND THE WORLD.
ARCTIC OCEAN
EUROPE
ASIA
AFRICA
NORTH AMERICA
STH AMERICA
NEW HOLLAND (AUSTRALIA)
NORTH PACIFIC OCEAN
SOUTH PACIFIC OCEAN
INDIAN OCEAN
NORTH ATLANTIC OCEAN
SOUTH ATLANTIC OCEAN
SOUTHERN OCEAN
ANTARCTIC OCEAN
Equator
Explanation of the Tracks.
First Voyage
Second do
Third do
The direction is shown by the Arrows.
Longitude East from Greenwich
Longitude West from Greenwich
THE LONDON PRINTING AND PUBLISHING COMPANY

THE WORLD ON MERCATOR'S PROJECTION SHOWING CAPTAIN COOK'S VOYAGES ROUND THE WORLD

Table of the Chronological Progress of the Principal Geographical Discoveries by Europeans.

861 *Feroe Islands*—discovered about this time by a Scandinavian vessel.

871 *Iceland*—by some Norwegian chiefs, compelled to leave their native country; or before this, by a Scandinavian pirate, Naddodd.

950 *Greenland*—by the Icelanders.

1001 *Winenland or Vinland*—a part of the continent of America, is supposed to have been discovered by the Icelanders. The Icelandic chronicles are full and minute respecting this discovery.

1344 *Madeira*—discovery attributed to an Englishman, Robert Macham; it was revisited in 1419 by Juan Gonzalez and Tristan Vaz, Portuguese.

1345 *Canary Isles*—by some Genoese and Spanish seamen.

1364 *Guinea*—coast, by some seamen of Dieppe.

1418 *Porto Santo*—by Vaz and Zarco, Portuguese.

1419 *Madeira*—visited by the same navigators; called Madeira on account of its woods.

1434 *Cape Bojador* or *Nun*—doubled by the Portuguese.

1440 } *Senegal River*
1445 } —by the Portuguese

1446 *Cape Verd*—by Denis Fernandez, a Portuguese.

1448 Azores Islands—by Gonzallo Vello, a Portuguese.

1449 *Cape Verd Islands*—by Antonio de Noli, a Genoese in the service of Portugal.

1484 *Congo*—by the Portuguese, under Diego Cam.

1486 *Cape of Good Hope*—by Bartholomew Diaz.

1492 *Lucayos (*or *Bahama) Islands*—by Columbus. *San Salvador,* one of these islands, was first seen by this great navigator, on the night of the 11th October.

Cuba, Island of Hispaniola
or
St. Domingo } by
1493 *Jamaica* } Columbus
St Christopher's }
Dominica }

1497 *Cape of Good Hope*—doubled by Vasco di Gama, and the passage to India discovered.

Newfoundland—by John Cabot.

1498 *Continent of America*—by Columbus.

Malabar, coast of—by Vasco di Gama.

1498 *Mozambique, Island of*—by Vasco di Gama.

1499 *America, eastern coasts of*—by Ojede and Amerigo Vespucci. (It is contended by some that this preceded by a year the discovery of the American continent by Columbus.)

1500 *Brazil*—24th April, by Alvarez de Cabral, a Portuguese, who was driven on its coasts by a tempest.

1501 *Labrador and River St. Lawrence*—by Cortecal, for the Portuguese.

1502 *Gulf of Mexico*—Some of the shores explored by Columbus, on his last voyage.

St. Helena, the Island of—by Jean de Nova, a Portuguese.

1506 *Ceylon*—by the Portuguese. (Ceylon was known to the Romans in the time of Claudius.)

1506 *Madagascar, Island of*—visited by Tristan da Cunha, and revisited by the Portugese navigator Fernandez Pereira, in 1508.

1508 *Canada*—visited by Thomas Aubert. Known before to fishermen.

Ascension Isle—by Tristan da Cunha

Sumatra, Island of—by Siqueyra, a Portuguese.

1511 *Molucca Isles*—by the Portuguese.

Sunda Isles—by Abrew, a Portuguese.

1512 *Maldives*—by a Portugese navigator.

Florida—by Ponce de Leon, a Spanish navigator.

1513 *Borneo and Java*—The Portuguese became acquainted with these islands.

South Sea—The Great Ocean was discovered this year from the mountains of Darien, by Nugnez de Balboa, and subsequently navigated by Magellan.

1515 *Peru*—by Perez de la Rua.

1516 *Rio de Janeiro*—by Dias de Solis.

Rio de la Plata—by the same.

1517 *China*—discovery of, by sea, by Fernandez Perez d'Andrada.

Bengal—by some Portuguese thrown on the coast by a tempest.

1518 *Mexico*—by the Spaniards. Conquered by Cortez in 1519.

1519 *Magellan, straits of*—passed by Magellan with a fleet of discovery, fitted out by the Emperor Charles V. The first voyage round the world was undertaken by this navigator; and his vessel performed the enterprise, although the commander perished.

1520 *Terra del Fuego*—by Magellan.

1521 *Ladrone Islands*—by Magellan.

Philippines—by Magellan, who lost his life here in a skirmish.

1524 *Canada* or *New France*—nominally taken possession of by Verrazzani, for Frans I. of France.

North America—travelled over from Florida to Newfoundland by Verrazzani, a Florentine, in the service of France.

1525 *Australia* or *New Holland*—Some parts discovered by the Portuguese, others by the Dutch, Spanish and English, in later years.

1527 *New Guinea*—by Saavedra, a Spaniard, sent from Mexico, by Cortez.

1530 *Guinea*—the first voyage to, made by an English ship for Elephant's teeth.

1534 *Canada*—visited by Cortier, of St. Malo.

1535 *California*—by Cortez.

1537 *Chili*—by Diego de Almagro, one of the conquerors of Peru.

1541 *Labrador*—by a French engineer, Alphonze.

India—the first English ship sailed to, for the purpose of attacking the Portuguese.

1542 *Japan*—by the Portuguese.

1545 *Potosi, mines of*—by the Spaniards.

1552 *Spitzbergen*—observed by the English.

1553 *White Sea*—by Chancellor, the discovery.

English navigator.

Nova Zembla—by Willoughby, an English sea-man.

1575 *Solomon's Isles*—by Mendana, a Spaniard.

1576 *Frobisher's Strait*—by the English navigator, Frobisher.

Greenland—further explored by Frobisher.

1577 *New Albion*—discovered by Drake, who was the second to attempt a voyage round the world, which he performed in three years.

1580 *Siberia*—discovered by Yermak Timopheievitch, chief of Cossacks.

1587 *Davis' Strait*—by the English navigator whose name it bears.

1594 *Falkland Islands*—by the English navigator, Hawkins.

1596 *Marquesas*—by Mendana, a Spaniard.

Solitary Island—by Mendana.

1606 *Archipelago del Espirito Santo*—the Cyclades of Bougainville, and the New Hebrides of Cook—by Guiros, a Portuguese.

Otahiete—supposed to be dis covered by Guiros, who named it Sagittaria.

1607 *Hudson's Bay*—by Hudson,
1610 on his third voyage.

1607 *Chesapak Bay*—by John Smith.

1615 *Straits of Le Maire* and the *Island of Staten*—by Le Maire, a merchant of Amsterdam, and Schouten, a merchant of Horn.

1616 *Cape Horn*—doubled by Le Maire and Schouten, Dutch navigators, who called it after the town of which Schouten was a native.

Van Diemen's Land—by Tasman, the Dutch navigator.

Baffin's Bay—by William Baffin, an Englishman.

1636 *Frozen Ocean*—by the Russians.

1642 *New Zealand*—by Tasman.

1654 *Bourbon, Isle of*—by the French.

1673 *Louisiana*—by the French.

1686 *Easter Island*—by Roggewein, a Dutch navigator.

1690 *Kamschatka*—by a Cossack chief, Morosko.

1692 *Japan*—visited by Kemfer, a German.

1699 *New Britain,* and the straits which separate it from New Guinea—discovered by Dampier.

1711 *Kurile Isles*—occupied by the Russians.

1728 *Behring's Strait*—explored and designated by a Danish navigator in the service of Russia, whose name it bears.

1741 *Aleutian Isles*—by Behring.

1765 *Duke of York's Island* and *Isles of Danger*—by Byron.

1767 *Otahiete*—by Wallis, an Englishman.

1768 *Cook's Strait*—by Captain Cook.

1770 *New South Wales*—by Captain Cook.

1772 *Island of Desolation*—by Kerguelen and by Cook.

1774 *New Caledonia*
1778 *Icy Cape* by Cook
Sandwich Islands

1797 *Bass's Straits*—by Mr. Bass, Surgeon of H.M.S. 'Reliance'.

1804, 5, 6 *Missouri* explored to its sources by Captains Lewis and Clarke.

1819 *Barrow's Straits*—by Lieut. Parry.

New South Shetland—by Mr. Smith, of the brig 'William.'

WESTERN HEMISPHERE
North Pole
South Pole
ARCTIC OCEAN
NORTH AMERICA
SOUTH AMERICA
NORTH PACIFIC OCEAN
SOUTH PACIFIC OCEAN
NORTH ATLANTIC OCEAN
SOUTH ATLANTIC OCEAN
ANTARCTIC OCEAN
CARIBBEAN SEA
GULF OF MEXICO
Tropic of Cancer
Equator or Equinoctial Line
Tropic of Capricorn
Antarctic Circle
Aleutian Isles
Sandwich Is.
Marquesas Is.
Low Archipelago
Society Is.
Navigators Is.
Friendly Is.
New Hebrides
New Caledonia
Solomons
Kermadec Is.
NEW ZEALAND
Galapagos
Falkland Is.
South Shetland Is.
SOUTH VICTORIA
Azores
Cape Verd Is.
Bermudas

Western Hemisphere

EASTERN HEMISPHERE
ARCTIC OCEAN
EUROPE
RUSSIAN EMPIRE
SIBERIA
ASIA
INDEPENDENT TARTARY
CHINESE EMPIRE
THIBET
ARABIA
AFRICA
SAHARA
ATLANTIC OCEAN
SOUTH ATLANTIC OCEAN
GULF OF GUINEA
INDIAN OCEAN
ARABIAN SEA
BAY OF BENGAL
Equator or Equinoctial Line
Tropic of Capricorn
Tropic of Cancer
NORTH PACIFIC OCEAN
CHINA SEA
AUSTRALASIA
AUSTRALIA
NEW SOUTH WALES
PAPUA OR NEW GUINEA
SOUTHERN OCEAN
Antarctic Circle
ANTARCTIC OCEAN
The Mail Route is Coloured thus

Eastern Hemisphere

EUROPE.
ARCTIC OCEAN
NORTH ATLANTIC OCEAN
NORTH SEA
BLACK SEA
MEDITERRANEAN SEA
ASIA
AFRICA
ASIA MINOR
SEAL HUNTING
LAPLAND TRAVELLERS
RUSSIAN TRAVELLERS
ARAB & CAMEL
SLAVE MARKET
SCALE
Longitude West 5 from Greenwich
Longitude East 20 from Greenwich

Europe

AREA AND PHYSICAL ASPECT

The most favoured and civilized division of the globe, Europe stretches from the Atlantic to the Ouralian Mountains, and from the Arctic Ocean to the Mediterranean; and at about 3,000,000 square miles it constitutes a sixteenth part of the terrestrial surface of the earth. A great plain extends from Holland eastward towards the Ouralian Mountains where the land rises in successive *steppes,* and much of this region is so low that if the waters of the Atlantic rose 1500 ft above their present level, the whole of Northern Europe, excepting the mountainous districts of Norway would be submerged. The southern part of Europe is more or less elevated, the highest mountain being Mont Blanc, which is 15,781 feet above sea level.

SEAS, LAKES AND RIVERS

The number and extent of the inland seas in Europe have greatly contributed to its civilization. The Mediterranean, including the two great inlets of the Adriatic and the Aegean or Archipelago, covers 800,000 square miles. Its rich coast line numerous islands, and delicious climate render this inland lake the finest navigable water in the world. Among the other important seas are the Black Sea, covering 230,000 square miles, the Baltic, covering 150,000 square miles, where the average depth is 60 fathoms, the White Sea in Northern Russia, which is but little known, and the North Sea, a part of the great Atlantic Ocean. There are many lakes, the largest being Ladoga and Onega in Russia. The main rivers are the Volga, Dnieper, Danube, Don, Rhine, Loire, Elbe, Rhône, Seine, Ebro, Po, Thames, Shannon, Severn and Clyde. The numerous seas, gulfs, bays, lakes and rivers are the means of supplying Europe with a larger quantity and a greater variety of fish than anywhere else in the world. The most valuable of the piscatory tribe is the herring.

CLIMATE

The greater part of Europe is within the temperate zone between the parallels of 35° and 60°. Owing probably to the extent of water, to the more general habitation, clearing and cultivation of the country, the northern parts of Europe are much cooler than similar latitudes in America.

POPULATION

Europe was originally inhabited by the Celts in the West and South, by the Finns in the North East and by the Laps in the furthest North. The Scythians or Goths from Asia drove the Celts before them, and their descendants now occupy the greatest portion of Europe. Other Asiatic peoples, the Sarmatian or Sclavonian, and their relatives the Heruli, also entered Europe, and have remained mainly in the east. One thousand years ago Northern, Central and Eastern Europe were thinly populated. In 1828 Malte Brun estimated the inhabitants of Europe at 205,000,000. By 1850 this figure may have reached 250,000,000, which means 83 mouths to each square mile. Most governments take the form of kingdoms, principalities or duchies. The chief religious groupings are: Roman Catholics, Protestants, Greek and Jew in the ratio approximately 122, 52, 43 and 2.

THE BRITISH ISLES
LONDON.
EDINBURGH
DUBLIN
SHETLAND ISLANDS
ORKNEY ISLANDS
HEBRIDES OR WESTERN ISLES
NORTH SEA
IRISH SEA
ST. GEORGES CHANNEL
BRISTOL CHANNEL
ENGLISH CHANNEL
CARDIGAN BAY
CHANNEL ISLANDS
FRANCE
DURHAM
SUFFOLK
SCALE
Meridian of Greenwich

The British Isles

Physical Aspect

Favourably situated in the Atlantic Ocean on the western side of Europe, the United Kingdom of Great Britain and Ireland is 600 miles long, 370 miles at its widest and has a circuit of about 3,000 miles. The southern parts of England and Wales are flat or undulating, while northern districts and southern Scotland are elevated. Wales, North Scotland and parts of Ireland are bold and mountainous. The scenery throughout the kingdom is very diversified, and (like so many islands adjoining continents) it contains in comparative miniature the leading features of the adjacent mainland.

Rivers and Harbours

The principal navigable streams are the Thames, Severn, Humber, Mersey and Tyne in England, the Tay, Tweed, Clyde and Solway in Scotland, and the Shannon in Ireland. Every part of the coast can boast numerous harbours, especially on the western shores. No region could be better adapted for extensive maritime traffic.

Transport

Throughout the kingdom there is a total of 87 canals, running some 2,300 miles. In England and Wales the length of the roads is 150,000 miles, of which 20,000 are turnpike roads, while in Scotland there are 3,500 of turnpike roads and the figure for Ireland is not known. 5,000 miles of railway are open, on which 60,000,000 passengers travel a year. In 1847, 52 passengers were killed, of whom 22 caused their own destruction.

History

The Celtic peoples who supposedly colonized the islands from the adjacent continent in 1000 BC were driven into Wales, Cornwall and Scotland by subsequent invasions of Romans and Anglo Saxons. Since the Norman conquest there has been a successive hereditary monarchy, excepting the interregnum of Cromwell.

Population

The English, Welsh, Scotch and Irish together number about 30,000,000, each possessing marked peculiarities. Education is conducted in national, British and Foreign, and Sunday schools; and more or less all children between seven and twelve years of age are in the course of instruction. The annual income of all people in the United Kingdom amounts to 500 million. The number of paupers relieved is over 2 million.

Trade and Industry

The declared value of United Kingdom produce exported in 1847 was fifty millions, of which over thirty were manufactures of cotton, wool and linen. The chief imports were corn, sugar, tea, coffee, raw wool and cotton, rum, wine, tobacco, timber and spices. There are 15,000 merchant sailing vessels with a total tonnage of 3 million, and 500 steam-vessels. Mining raises 30 million tons of coal and 1 million of iron annually. Aside from cloth production, the chief industries are those of hardware and cutlery, and leather. Also 30 million gallons of spirits are distilled, and 8 million barrels of beer brewed.

Foreign Possessions

The area of British foreign possessions throughout the world (exclusive of the Hudson's Bay territories in North America) is upwards of 2,000,000 square miles, which contain about 120,000,000 subjects of the British crown. To these may be added tributary and dependent states whose inhabitants number at least 50,000,000.

The Illustrations by H. Warren & Engraved by J. Rogers.

The Map Drawn & Engraved by J. Rapkin.

England and Wales

Area and Physical Aspect

This portion of the United Kingdom, bounded by the North Sea to the east, the English Channel to the south, the Irish Sea to the west and by Scotland to the North, is triangular in form, England and Wales offer a variety of landscape: in the east, broad plains clothed with the richest verdure; in the south gentle undulations with waving woods and fertile cornfields; in the west, hills and sloping vales affording pasturage to innumerable herds of sheep; and in the north, mountain and dell, craggy ravines and bleak moors. But almost everywhere is cultivated like a garden and studded with happy homes, from princely castles to neat cottages; the whole presenting a *coup d'oeil* such as no experienced traveller can contemplate without admiration and delight.

Mountains

The Cumberland hills, which have been termed the British Appenines, pass through Westmoreland and Yorkshire to Derbyshire and are rich in mineral wealth. The Welsh mountains consist rather of elevated peaks rising out of table lands than of continuous ridges, Snowden, Plinlimmon and Cadair Idris being the most conspicuous.

Climate

Estimated by the number of days in the year that a man may work in the open air, by the variety of vegetation and the average duration of life, England has the finest climate in the world. The mean heat is from 50° to 53° Fahrenheit, the range from 22° to 82°.

Minerals

The land is rich in various ores, including iron, copper, lead and tin. It has been estimated that in South Wales alone there is sufficient coal to supply England for 2,000 years after all the other mines are exhausted. There are various mineral springs at such places as Bath, Buxton, Harrowgate, Cheltehham.

Population

The present number of inhabitants is about 18,000,000 of whom 2,000,000 live in London and its environs. The rate of increase has recently been reduced by extensive emigration. The Protestant church is established by law and is supervised by two archbishops and 25 bishops. The total number of ecclesiastical benefices with and without cure of souls is 10,540. Education is very extensive, and it is estimated that 1,000,000 children in England and Wales are educated in private schools as paying scholars, with a further 1,500,000 in charitable schools of various kinds. For the purposes of administration, England is divided into 42 counties, and Wales into 12. The total number of electors registered in both counties and boroughs is 856,438.

Commerce and Industry

The coasting trade between the different ports of the United Kingdom has increased from nine to thirteen million tons in twelve years. There are over 33,800 ships trading with foreign ports, the official value of British and Irish produce exported in 1846 being £132,250,000. The increase in steam vessels is extraordinary, numbers having risen from 59 in 1821 to 963 in 1846. There are 72 joint-stock banks and 211 private banks authorized to issue paper money and the total coin in circulation is about £30,000,000. Revenue is raised by taxes on property, soap, bricks, paper, spirits, etc.

The Illustrations by J. Marchant & Engraved by J. Rogers.

The Map Drawn & Engraved by J. Rapkin.

JOHN TALLIS & COMPANY, LONDON & NEW YORK.

Ireland

Area and Physical Aspect

Bounded on the north, west and south by the Atlantic Ocean, and on the east by St George's Channel and the Irish Sea, Ireland comprises an area of 32,433 square miles. The face of the country is picturesquely varied, although more than 6,000,000 acres consist of unimproved mountain and bog. In the Bog of Allen, which occupies 77,000 acres, the aspect is bleak and hopelessly barren The principal mountain ranges run from north, to south with the highest elevation at 3,410 feet in Macgillicuddy's Reeks. Less than a fourth part of the surface is employed in supplying food for 8,000,000 people. It has been ascertained that 100 tons of peat, or bog, may at the expense of £20 be made to yield over £91 in various gases and other products.

Lakes and Rivers

Lakes or Loughs are numerous and cover 467,577 acres. The Lakes of Killdeer are famous for their beauty. The principal streams consist of the Shannon, Barrow, Blackwater, Bann, Boyne, Liffey, Lee and Foyle, of which the Shannon is unsurpassed for magnitude and extent of inland navigation by any river in the United Kingdom.

Cities and Towns

Dublin, the capital (population 250,000), is well situated and in its buildings, squares and streets is not inferior to London. Cork (population 100,000) is famed for its extensive cove and verdant hills, but the city has few fine buildings. Belfast is the Liverpool of Ireland and has a population of nearly 100,000.

History

The traditional annals of Ireland extend to remote antiquity and there is abundant evidence that the island was at a very early period in a high state of civilization. It is likely that the island received the light of Christianity before Britain, direct from the eastern churches. In 1171 several of the kings and bishops of Ireland swore fealty to Henry II of England, and after centuries of difficulties caused by the existence of separate legislatures in the two countries, an effective union between England and Ireland finally took place in 1800.

Commerce and Industry

The linen trade is the staple manufacture of Ireland and employs half a million people, with 600 million yards exported annually. The value of imports and exports has risen from 10 million pounds sterling at the time of union in 1800 to £40,000,000 in 1848.

Government

The country is divided into four provinces, Ulster, Munster, Leinster and Connaught, which are in turn divided into thirty-two counties. Ireland has been exempted from many of the taxes paid in England and Scotland, paying no property or income tax, no duty on stage carriages or railways, no taxes on soap, hops, servants, windows, etc. In 1840 four poor law unions were established, a charter of justice which has existed in England since the sixteenth century, but is only now being carried into effect in Ireland. Education is rapidly extending, and parliament grants £100,000 annually for the national schools and has made a similar sum available to build three new colleges solely for secular education. Trinity College in Dublin was endowed by Queen Elizabeth.

SCOTLAND
EDINBURGH.
BRIG OF DOON & BURNS MONUMENT.
SCOTT'S MONUMENT.
DEER STALKING.
HOLYROOD HOUSE.
SHINTY.
SHETLAND ISLES
ORKNEY ISLES
PENTLAND FIRTH
CAITHNESS
SUTHERLAND
CROMARTY
ROSS
INVERNESS
ABERDEEN
PERTH
ARGYLL
FIRTH OF FORTH
FIRTH OF TAY
MORAY FIRTH
DORNOCH FIRTH
SOLWAY FIRTH
FIRTH OF CLYDE
NORTH CHANNEL
THE MINCH
LITTLE MINCH
HEBRIDES OR WESTERN ISLES
ATLANTIC OCEAN
NORTH SEA
ENGLAND
IRELAND
ISLE OF MAN
SCALE.
Longitude W. West from Greenwich
The Illustrations by H. Whittock & Engraved by J. Rogers
The Map Drawn & Engraved by J. Rapkin.
JOHN TALLIS & COMPANY, LONDON & NEW YORK.

Scotland

Area and Physical Aspect

Bounded on the north by the North Sea and Pentland Firth, on the east by the German Ocean, on the west by the Atlantic Ocean and on the south by England and the Irish Sea, Scotland is exceedingly varied in aspect. Two-thirds of the surface is mountainous and not above one-eighth is cultivated, the remainder being devoted to pasturage. Naturally divided into the highland and Lowland areas, the country is grand, imposing but bleak in the north, with dangerous rocky coasts on the west, and more highly cultivated and picturesque in the south. The construction of a harbour at Peterhead on the east coast has greatly mitigated the perils incurred by Scotch seafarers. Deep indentations in the coast cause wide variations in the total breadth from 160 miles to only 24 miles across from east to west. The main mountain ranges are the Grampians, the Lead Hills, the Pentland, Lammermuir, and the Cheviot Hills on the confines of England. The highest peak is Ben Nevis in Inverness-shire at 4,370 feet. The climate is rigorous, cold in the north and humid in the south.

Lakes, Rivers and Inland Navigation

There are many beautiful lakes, or lochs, and fine rivers abounding in fish, especially salmon and trout. Loch Lomond in Dumbartonshire stands pre-eminent among the lakes for its lovely scenery. The chief rivers are the Tay, Tweed, Spey, Clyde, Dee and Forth. The Great or Clyde Canal was begun in 1768 to connect the Clyde with the Forth, and the Caledonian Canal, which has cost over a million sterling to build, links the Atlantic and the Moray Firth.

History

Anciently possessed by the rival nations of Scots in the west and Picts in the east, the kingdom of Scotland was formed in 845 and remained independent until its King James VI ascended the English throne over 750 years later. It is now divided into 34 counties, returning a total of 683 members.

Chief Cities

Edinburgh, the capital, is justly famed for its fine position and noble buildings. Glasgow is the great trading mart of Scotland and, with the neighbouring towns on the Clyde, is the chief seat of manufactures. Dundee and Aberdeen are well known for their flax manufactures.

Population

Numbers have been increasing but slowly, from just over 1,000,000 in 1700, to 1,649,000 in 1801, and 2,620,184 in 1841. Education is universal and good. The Scotch are deeply religious, most being Presbyterian, although there are many Roman Catholics in the north and south of the country. They are still strongly attached to feudal customs and remain devoted to the heads of clans or families in their respective localities.

Commerce and Industry

The number of people engaged in agricultural work only just exceeds the number employed in commerce, trade and manufacture. Coal, iron and lead abound and are widely mined. There is not one private banker left in Scotland, the whole monetary transactions of the country being carried on by joint-stock banks, of which there are six chartered and fifteen unchartered.

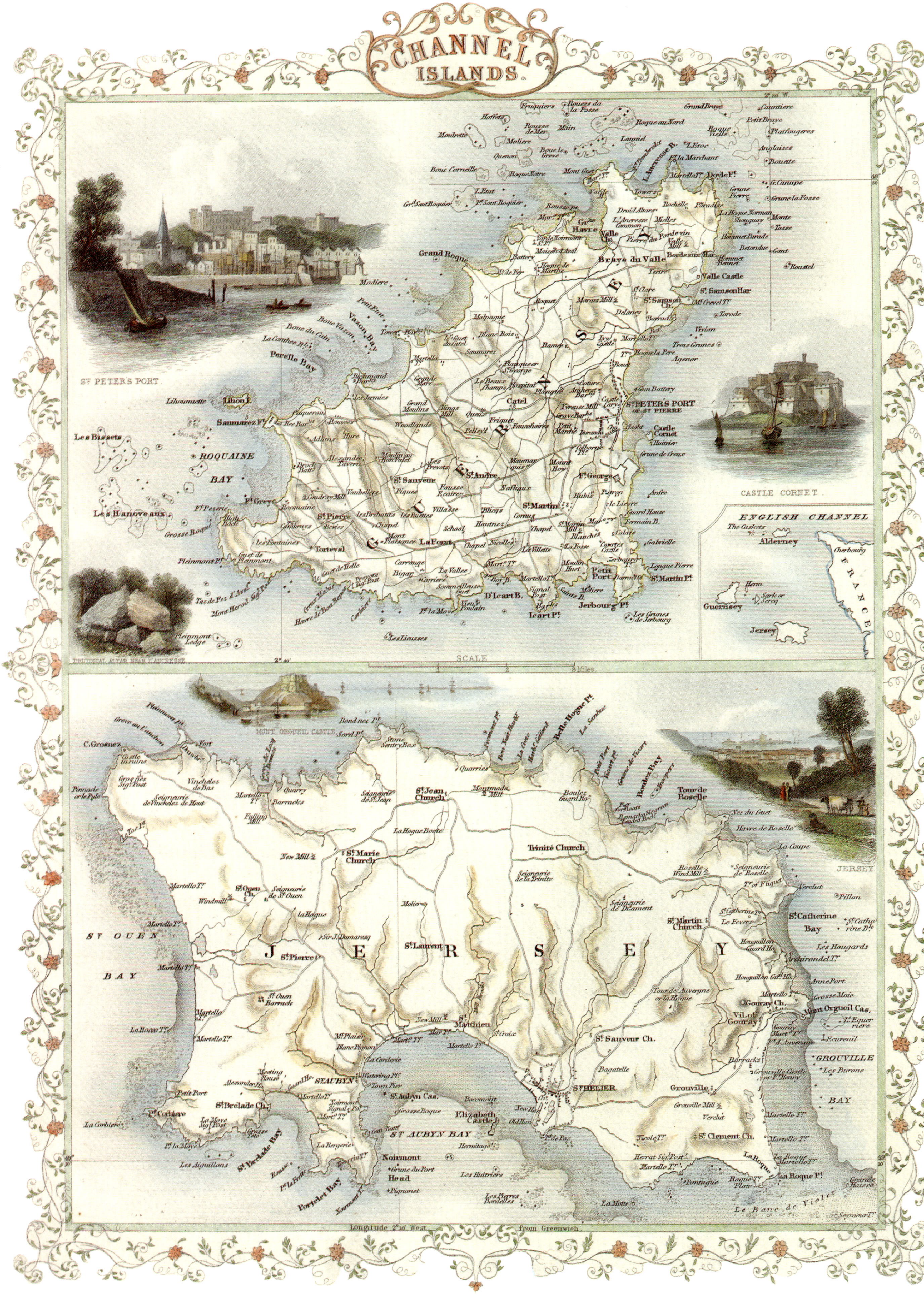
CHANNEL ISLANDS.
GUERNSEY
ST PETER'S PORT
CASTLE CORNET
DRUIDICAL ALTAR NEAR L'ANCRESSE
ENGLISH CHANNEL
Alderney
Guernsey
Herm
Sark or Sercq
Jersey
FRANCE
St PETER'S PORT or St PIERRE
Castle Cornet
ROQUAINE BAY
Perelle Bay
Vason Bay
Grand Roque
Braye du Valle
Valle Castle
St Sampson Har
St Martin
Jerbourg Pt
Icart Pt
Les Hanoveaux
Les Bissets
Lihou I.
Pleinmont Pt
SCALE
JERSEY
J E R S E Y
MONT ORGUEIL CASTLE
St OUEN BAY
St AUBYN BAY
GROUVILLE BAY
St Catherine Bay
St HELIER
St AUBYN
Elizabeth Castle
St Brelade Ch.
St Brelade Bay
Portelet Bay
Noirmont Head
La Corbière
Trinité Church
St Jean Church
St Martin Church
St Laurent
St Pierre
St Sauveur Ch.
St Clement Ch.
Grouville
Mont Orgueil Cas.
Tour de Roselle
Bouley Bay
C. Grosnez
Le Banc de Violet
Longitude 2° 10' West from Greenwich

Channel Islands

JERSEY, GUERNSEY, ALDERNY, SERK, HERM and JEDTHOU are the largest of this group of islands lying near the coast of France. Since William the Conqueror attached them as a fief to the English crown they have remained loyal and integral parts of the dominion of this realm.

JERSEY was anciently called Caesurea. The island is situated almost 13 miles from the coast of France in the English Channel. Around 12 miles long and 5 to 6 miles wide, it slopes from a rocky and precipitous coast in the north to a fertile alluvial belt abounding in rich orchards and fruitful fields. St. Heliers, the chief town, has airy streets and excellent markets, and is well protected. Druidical monuments are evidence that Jersey was peopled by a Celtic race before being occupied by the Romans for a considerable period, and then by the Normans. The population has more than doubled since 1806 and now stands at about 50,000, of whom 30,000 or so live in St. Heliers. This increase can be dated to the establishment of weekly intercourse by steam with the mother country in 1824, and shortly afterwards with France. The protestant faith is universal among the native inhabitants, although there are Roman Catholics among the the Irish and aliens living on the island. The laws of the island are based on an original charter granted to Jersey by King John, now slightly modified by various orders of the English sovereigns. The States, or legislative assembly, consists of the governor, representing the sovereign, the bailli, and 36 representatives of the local parishes. Repeated attempts by the French to conquer Jersey have necessitated the maintenance of a well-trained militia and several strongholds.

GUERNSEY is situated within sight of the French coast. This triangular island was named La bien heureuse Ile Sainte by the monks who came to it in AD 996. The southern coast is broken into picturesque bays with rocky headlands. The land shelves towards the north, where fine sandy beaches are rendered almost inaccessible by a chain of rocks. The chief town is St Peter's Port, is built on a steep acclivity forming a natural amphitheatre (population about 17,000).

The people of both islands are marked by their courage, shrewdness and honesty. norman French is spoken but English is becoming very general. Agriculture and the rearing of excellent horned cattle are carried to great perfection in both islands.

ALDERNEY lies 21 miles north-east of Guernsey. The island is 4 miles long and 1 mile wide. Bounded on the south and west by cliffs 100 to 200 feet high, it is beset by rocks which extend to form a chain, the Caeskets, on which a fine lighthouse is built. The population numbers about 2,000. Half the island is cultivated, the other half pasturage.

SERK lies 6 miles east of Guernsey, and is only 3 miles long and 1 in breadth. The population is about 600. Herme and Jedthou are very small and used only for feeding cattle.

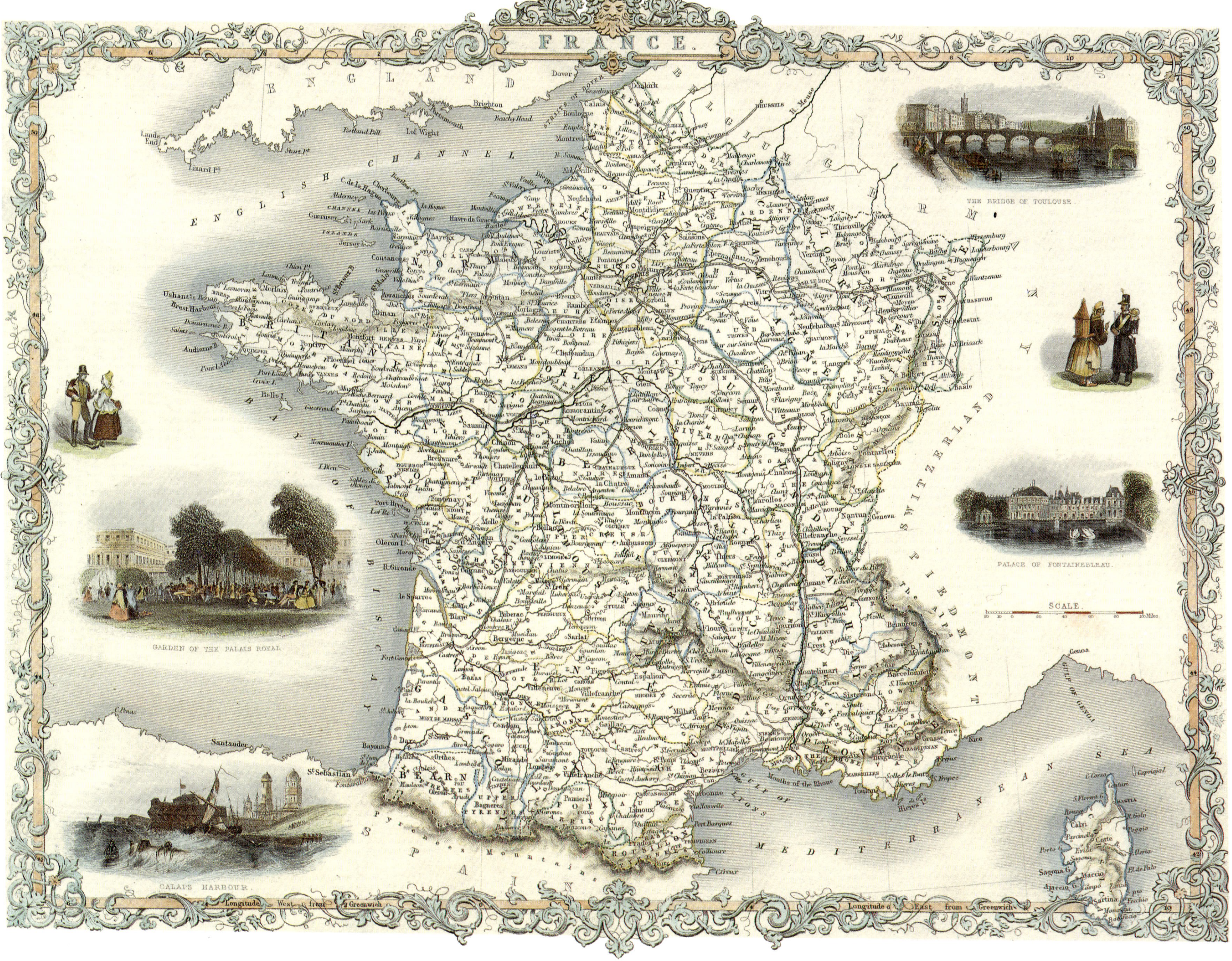
FRANCE.
ENGLAND
ENGLISH CHANNEL
STRAITS OF DOVER
BELGIUM
GERMANY
SWITZERLAND
PIEDMONT
BAY OF BISCAY
SPAIN
MEDITERRANEAN SEA
GULF OF LYONS
GULF OF GENOA
Pyrenees Mountains
THE BRIDGE OF TOULOUSE.
PALACE OF FONTAINEBLEAU.
GARDEN OF THE PALAIS ROYAL.
CALAIS HARBOUR.
SCALE
Longitude West from Greenwich
Longitude East from Greenwich

France

Area and Physical Aspect

This ancient kingdom, nearly hexagonal in shape, has an area of 200,000 square miles. Leval or slightly undulating in the north and centre, its highest lands lie to the east and south. Chief mountain ranges are the Cevennes, west of the Rhône, the Vosges, on the German border, the Jura and the Alps on the confines of Switzerland, and the Pyrennees. Of 52,000,000 hectares of surface, 22,800,000 are arable and 7,000,000 pasture with the richest soil in the north. Coal and iron abound in various parts and there are numerous mineral springs. The variety of climate, from the north which is similar to that of England but drier, to the warmer south, marks the division in vegetation for the production of the vine, olive, maize and corn.

Rivers and Canals

There are an estimated 6,000 rivers, the chief of these being the Rhône, Loire, Garonne and Seine. The Loire is the longest and is navigable to Paris, even for large-sized boats, and to Rouen for masted vessels. The Canal du Midi unites the Atlantic with the Mediterranean. There are few harbours, and none of those in the English Channel are good.

History

France was known under Roman dominance as Transalpine Gaul, an area that also included Helvetia (now Switzerland) and that part of Germany which lies west of the Rhine. In the fifth century AD, the Franks crossed the Rhine from Germany, conquered Gaul and laid the foundations of an empire which reached its peak of power and prosperity under Charlemagne. After William, duke of Normandy, made himself king of England in 1066, France became involved in almost perpetual wars with that nation over many centuries. The present emperor, styled Napoleon III, is nephew of Bonaparte.

Population and Divisions

In 1790 France was divided into 83 departments, each of which is subdivided into *arrondissements,* and these in turn into 2669 cantons. In 1827 the population was 31,851,545, of whom about 25,000,000 are French, the remainder Bretons, Basques, Germans, Jews and Gypsies. The Roman Catholic religion predominates and its clergy number about 37,000.

Cities and Towns

Paris, the capital (population 1,000,000), is favourably situated on the Seine, and is the gayest and in some respects the finest city in the world. There are magnificent public buildings, churches, palaces, museums, libraries, hospitals and other useful institutions. Next in size to Paris is Marseille (population 168,000), followed by Lyons (156,000) and Bordeaux (100,000).

Trade and Industry

Total manufactures are estimated at 1,800,000,000 francs or £75,000,000, of which silks, woollens, hemp, flax, lace and cotton make up tne chief part. The quantity of brandy and wine made is not known but must be very great, and estimated at 800,000,000 francs. Exports are valued at £38,500,000.

Foreign Possessions

These include Algiers, Senagal etc. in Africa; Martinique, Guadaloupe and Cayenne in the West Indies; St Pierre and Miguelore near Newfoundland; and several towns in India.

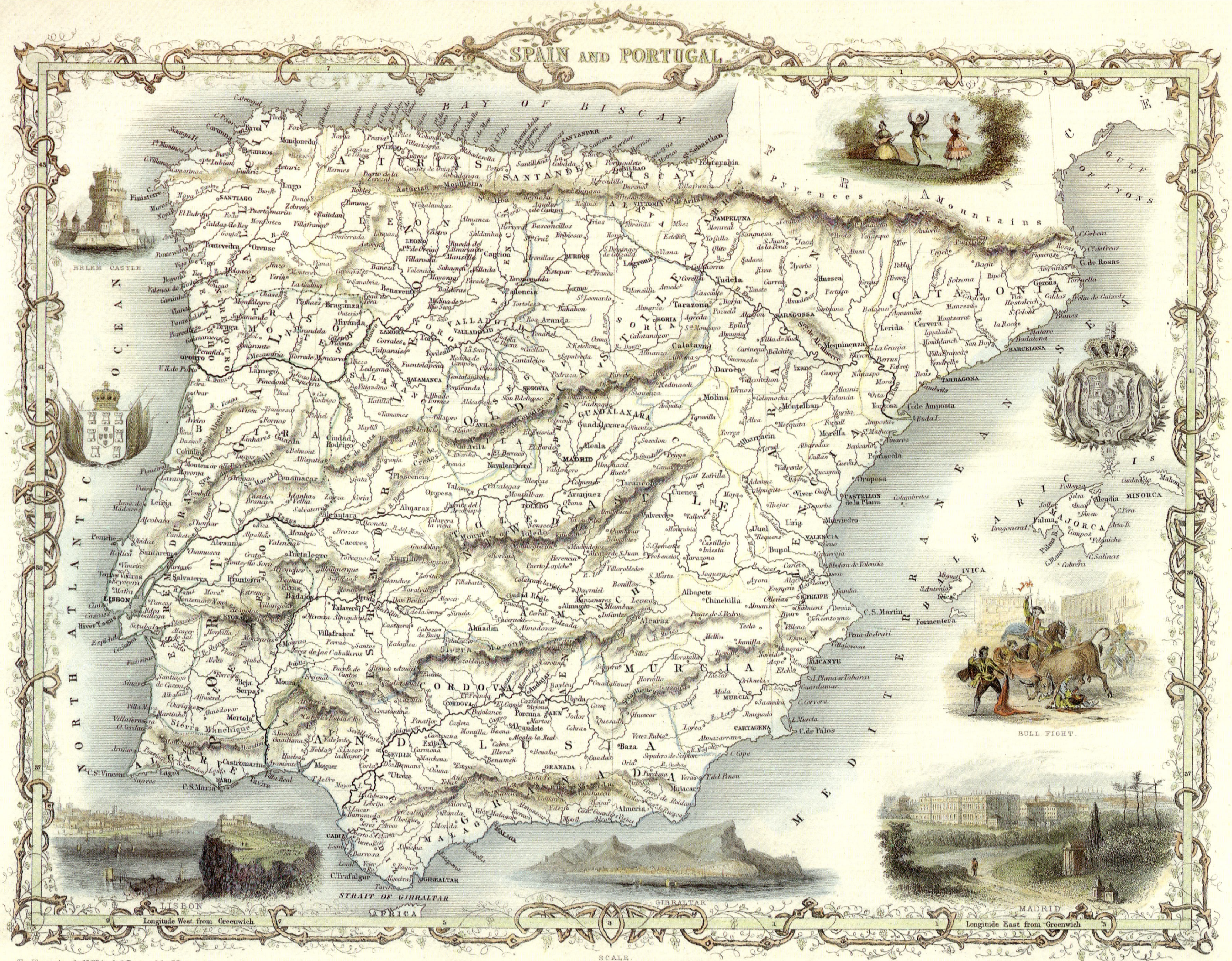

The Illustrations by H. Whitnock & Engraved by J. Rogers.

The Map Drawn & Engraved by J. Rapkin.

Spain and Portugal

Spain

Area and Physical Aspect

Five main mountain ranges intersect the country, with great plains and elevated table-land between, and there are 230 rivers, few of them navigable.

History

After 400 years as a Roman province, Spain was conquered by the Visigoths. The Moors then invaded and established prosperous possessions in the south. They were expelled in the thirteenth century. Columbus added vast territories in America to the Spanish dominions but in 1823-5 most of these were lost. Now a hereditary sovereignty divided into 12 provinces, with a Cortes, or representative assembly, although the Basque provinces and Navarre retain their ancient laws.

Chief Cities

Madrid, the capital (population 200,000), is a handsome city built on an elevated plain. The Escurial, 22 miles north-west of Madrid is one of the largest palaces in the world. The port of Barcelona (120,000) is the commercial capital of the country.

Population

Now estimated at between 13 and 14 millions, the Spaniards are a proud race, Roman Catholic by religion. Education is very imperfect for the mass of the people, although there are 15 universities.

Trade and Industry

Spain is rich in mineral wealth, particularly quicksilver, cinnabar, lead and coal. Much of the land is owned by the nobility and the clergy and large areas are swampy or otherwise unusable. Most of Spain's foreign trade is with England and France, though that is on a small scale.

Portugal

Area and Physical Aspect

360 miles long and 120 wide, Portugal is divided into six provinces. Known as Lusitania when inhabited by the Celts, it was conquered by the Romans and for many centuries followed the fate and fortunes of Spain. Since 1640, however, it has been an independent monarchy. Mainly mountainous and rocky, Portugal has few harbours though the two largest rivers, the Tagus and the Douro, offer good inland navigation.

Chief Cities

Lisbon, the capital (population 26,000,000), is built on the banks of the Tagus where the river is 9 miles broad, and would shelter 10,000 sail of vessels. In 1755 much of the city was destroyed by an earthquake, but now it has a picturesque appearance. Oporto (population 70,000), built on the Douro, has a good harbour and a considerable trade.

Population

The total number is estimated at 4,200,000. They differ from the Spaniards in appearance, language and character. Roman Catholic in religion, it is said that every fifteenth person belongs to the sacerdotal order. Education is very defective, with only about 800 elementary schools.

Trade and Industry

50 per cent of Portuguese trade is with England, including 26,000,000 gallons of wine. Chief products of the country are corn, wine, oil, cork, drugs and fruit.

RUSSIA IN EUROPE
ARCTIC OCEAN
THE NEVSKOI PROSPECT, ST PETERSBURG
POLISH CAPTIVES ON THEIR WAY TO SIBERIA
TRAVELLING SLEDGE
RUSSIAN BEAR
NAPOLEON'S FLIGHT FROM MOSCOW
GULF OF OBE
Arctic Circle
WHITE SEA
ARCHANGEL
VOLOGDA
FINLAND
GULF OF FINLAND
ST PETERSBURG
SEA OF AZOF
BLACK SEA
CASPIAN SEA
ASIA MINOR
PERSIA
AUSTRIA
CONSTANTINOPLE
SCALE
Longitude East from Greenwich

Russia in Europe

AREA AND PHYSICAL ASPECT

The area of European Russia is separated from Asiatic Russia by the Ourralian Mountains. It extends from the Arctic Ocean to the Black Sea, and from the borders of Austria to Siberia. The greater part of the interior is a vast plain, with successive steppes of table-land to the southward. Vast tracts are covered with forest. Gold abounds in the Ouralian chain, also silver and copper. Iron is also plentiful, but coal is not known.

RIVERS, LAKES AND SEAS

The longest river, the Volga (1,7000 miles), is navigable from the Caspian to Tver. An extensive canal system also offers water communication in many directions. A traveller may pass from St Petersburg 4,124 miles to Siberia with only a few miles of porterage. There are numerous lakes, Ladoga the largest covering 7,200 square miles. The Arctic, White, Black, Caspian and Baltic Seas form an considerable water frontier.

CHIEF CITIES

Petersburg, the capital (population over 500,000), covers about 30 square miles on islands and mainland at the mouth of the river Neva. The former capital Moscow (population 300,000) is also of immense extent, the grand architecture being more Eastern than European. There are many other cities and fortresses in the empire, including the ports of Sevastopol, Odessa and Riga.

HISTORY

The chief founders of this great empire may be considered the Sclavonians and the Scandinavians who established the cities of Novgorod and Kiev. Further territories were acquired by the tzars Ivan the Great and Peter the Great, and the empress Catherine, who also founded many new cities. The invasion of Russia by Napoleon, and the subsequent destruction of the French army by cold, famine and the sword constitute one of the most fearful catastrophes in history.

POPULATION

Now about 60 millions, comprising 100 nations speaking 40 languages, the population is divided into four classes: nobility, clergy, freemen and serfs, these last being literally slaves who are bought and sold with the land which they cultivate. The established faith is that of the Greek church, introduced in 981 AD, though there are some 5,000,000 people of other religions. Government is despotic, and all power centres in the hereditary emperor who may consult his ministers at will. In the provinces the delegated authority of the emperor lies in a civil and a military governor.

TRADE AND INDUSTRY

The trade of Russia is very wide and varied, with active land traffic to other parts of Asia and Eastern Europe and marine trade elsewhere. In almost every instance the balance of trade is in favour of Russia. Iron and precious metals are extensively mined. There are several government manufactories of cloth and weapons. There are 7,000,000 sheep in the Crimea alone.

DEFENCE

The army is raised by conscription and numbers nearly one million men. The legal term of service is 25 years, the pay 1 1/3 *d*. per day and 150 lbs of meat and 44 lbs salt annually. There are, in addition, two naval divisions stationed in the Black Sea and three in the Baltic.

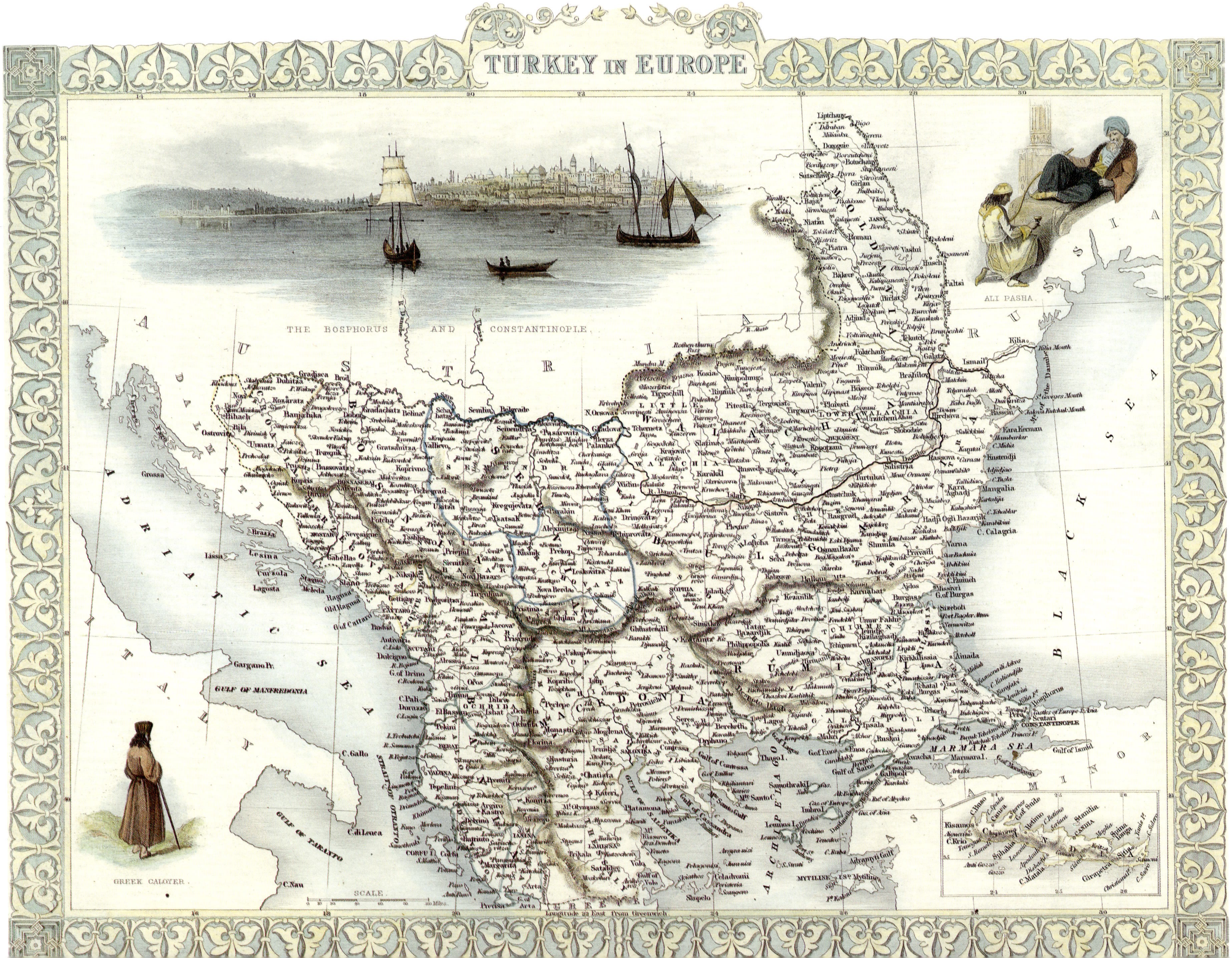
TURKEY IN EUROPE
THE BOSPHORUS AND CONSTANTINOPLE
ALI PASHA
GREEK CALOYER
AUSTRIA
RUSSIA
BLACK SEA
ADRIATIC SEA
ITALY
MOLDAVIA
WALLACHIA
SERVIA
BOSNIA
ALBANIA
MACEDONIA
RUMILI
BULGARIA
ARCHIPELAGO
MARMARA SEA
GULF OF MANFREDONIA
GULF OF TARANTO
STRAIT OF OTRANTO
DALMATIA
CONSTANTINOPLE
SCALE
Longitude 22 East from Greenwich

Turkey in Europe

Area and Physical Aspect

This fine country, which forms a portion of the dominions of the sultan, covers 180,000 square miles of some of the richest territory of Europe. It is diversified by mountains, valleys, forests, plains, rivers and arms of the sea. The chief mountain ranges are the Balkan, running east to west, whose highest peak, Orbelus, stands at 9,660 feet; and the Hellenic, running north to south. The rivers Danube, Maritza, Drin, Warda and other streams combine to render Turkey one of the best irrigated countries in Europe.

Climate

Temperate and naturally well-adapted for man; but the filthy habits and indolence, inevitably resulting from opium smoking' have caused Constantinople and other Moslem cities to be seats of pestilence; and a country that might have been the very garden of Europe is in many parts wild and uninhabitable.

History

The Turks, a Tartaric or Scythian race, migrated from Siberia and the Asian steppes in quest of a more fertile country. In the ninth and tenth centuries Turkish dynasties, having embraced Mahomedanism, reigned in Palestine, Syria and Egypt, later extending their dominions to Persia. Solyman I entered Europe across the Bosphorus in 1355, and successive sultans added further territories in Europe and Asia, finally conquering Constantinople, for over one thousand years the seat of Byzantine Christendom, in 1453. But for the gallantry of the Venetians, Hungarians and Poles who opposed them, the Turks would probably have overrun Europe, as they did a large part of Asia and Africa. Turkey in Europe now consists of several provinces, including Rumelia, Macedonia, Thessaly, Albania, Bosnia, Servia, and Bulgaria.

Chief Cities

Most favourably situated for the capital of a great empire, Constantinople (population nearly 900,000) is built upon hills, and three-fourths of it face the sea. Its mosques, painted houses and surrounding scenery combine to produce an effect not to be found in any other city in the world. Next in commercial importance is Salonika (population about 100,000), the capital of Macedonia and a city of imposing appearance with its domes and monuments.

Population

Estimations are vague, but Turkey in Europe is said to contain about 7,000,000 inhabitants of very varied race and character. Pure Turks account for less than half, with Greeks, Tartars, Armenians, Albanians, etc. making up the rest. The Turks have degenerated from their former manly character and will probably ere long be driven out of Europe. Government is entirely in the hands of the sultan, head of temporal and spiritual power and pope of the Mahomedans throughout the world. The provinces are governed by pachas, nominated by the sultan, and preserve their own local laws, taxes and customs.

Trade and Industry

Trade is small considering the great resources of the empire and the liberality of the Turkish tariff, which admits foreign goods at a very moderate percentage. Even so, in 1847 Britain exported more woollen and cotton goods to Turkey than to Russia, and imported corn, oil, fruits, silk, gums, drugs and dyes in return.

IONIAN ISLES AND GREECE.
TEMPLE OF JUPITER OLYMPUS AT ATHENS.
MODERN GREEK.
ANCIENT WAR CHARIOT.
GREEK CORSAIRS OFF CORFU.
NOTE.
Ionian Isles Coloured.
Longitude 23 East from Greenwich
SCALE.
TURKEY
MOREA
GRECIAN ARCHIPELAGO
GULF OF VOLO
GULF OF PATRAS
GULF OF LEPANTO
CHANNEL OF TALANTA
CHANNEL OF NEGROPONT
GULF OF EGINA
GULF OF NAPOLIA
GULF OF KOLOKYTHI
GULF OF KORON
GULF OF ARCADIA
CEPHALONIA
ZANTE
S. MAURA
ITHACA
SKIATHOS
SKOPELO
CELADRONI
SARAKINO
IPSERA
STAMPALIA
SYRA
MICONI
THERMIA
SERPHO
SIPHANTO
NAXIA
PARO
AMORGO
SANTORINI
ANAPHI
MILO
NIO
HYDRA
EGINA
ATHENS
CORINTH
PATRAS
LEPANTO
C. Matapan

Greece

Area and Physical Aspect

The modern kingdom of Greece, as settled by the European protocol of 1830, extends south of the Othrys mountains, and contains about 16,000 square miles. Mountain ridges, with isolated snow-capped peaks, table-lands, fertile valleys, numerous streams, inlets and coastal harbours constitute the principal features. Less than two-fifths of the country is capable of cultivation, but in picturesque scenery it is superior to every part of Europe, The famed Mount Parnassus is a peak of the Pindaric chain, while Mount Helicon, supposed abode of the muses, lies on the other side of the plain of Livadia.

Climate

With long hot summers and short severe winters, the range of thermometer is from 28° to 104° F.

History

Nearly 4,000 years ago Greece was inhabited by fierce savages. The foundation of Athens by an Egyptian around 3500 BC was followed over the succeeding two millennia by the parcelling out of the country among different kings or rulers. The rise, progress and decline of the various Grecian states as kingdoms, oligarchies and republics is well chronicled by ancient historians. Conquered by Rome, Greece became a province of that empire and was known as Achaia. Home to the earliest Christian churches, Greece was overrun by the Turks after the capture of Constantinople in 1453, and centuries of struggle for freedom from Moslem subjugation followed. In 1822-5 the sympathies of Europe were finally roused and with English, French and Russian aid Greece achieved independence. In 1831 Otho, son of the king of Bavaria, was elected king of Greece and is the present sovereign. A senate or legislative body is chosen every three years by the people.

Chief Cities

Modern Athens (population about 20,000) is built on part of the site of the ancient city. Many houses were destroyed during the war of independence. The Piraeus, or port of Athens, has a population of about 2,000.

Population

Greece must formerly have been densely populated. Attica is supposed to have contained 600 mouths to each square mile. The present population, including that of the islands, is about 1,000,000. The government is making considerable efforts for the education of the people, in which it is aided by missionaries from England and America. The Greek church owes its origin to the division of the Roman Empire into Oriental or Greek, and Occidental or Western. Despite subsequent attempts to reunite the Latin and Greek churches, the schism has ever since continued. Unlike the Romish church, Greek Christianity does not acknowledge the Pope as vicar of Christ, nor does it permit carved images, though paintings are sanctioned. The clergy may marry once, though monks and the higher clergy must remain celibate.

Trade and Industry

The trade of Piraeus does not employ more than 5,000 tons annually, though silk, oil, wine, grain and various minerals are produced and could be developed. Most trade is conducted with Turkey, Syria, Austria and France. At the present time the government is unable to meet even the interest on a large national debt.

AUSTRIA
ST STEPHENS, VIENNA.
RETURN OF THE SENNERIN.
VIENNA.
SCALE
Longitude East from 18 Greenwich
PRUSSIA
RUSSIA
GERMANY
SWITZERLAND
ITALY
TURKEY IN EUROPE
ADRIATIC SEA
BOHEMIA
MORAVIA
GALICIA
HUNGARY
TRANSYLVANIA
AUSTRIA
TYROL
LOMBARDY
SCLAVONIA
BANNAT
Riesen Gebirg
Bohemian Mountains
VENICE
VIENNA
Breslau
Oppeln
Dresden
Munich
Passau
Ratisbon
Salzburg
Innsbruck
Trieste
Milan
Mantua
Verona
Padua
Agram
Pest
Buda
Presburg
Debreczin
Szegedin
Temeswar
Hermanstadt
Kronstadt
Clausenburg
Lemberg
Tarnow
Czernowitz
Belgrade
Semlin
Ragusa
Cattaro
Spalatro
Zara
Lissa
Lesina
Curzola
Brazza
Lagosta
Meleda
Ancona
Ravenna
Bukarest
Krajova
Pitesti
River Danube

Austria

Area and Physical Aspect

The strangest aggregate of nations, the Austrian empire is bounded on the north by Russia, on the east by Turkey, on the south by the Adriatic, the duchies of Parma and Modena and the Papal States, and on the west by Switzerland and Bavaria. From west to east its greatest extent is about 900 miles, from north to south about 410 miles. The aspect of the Austrian empire differs from that of Europe in general by being mountainous rather than level. Elevated chains of mountains, noble rivers, numerous lakes and extensive rivers render the scenery strikingly picturesque.

History

The foundation of this powerful empire was laid in the time of Charlemagne and named the margravate of Austria. Over the succeeding centuries its fortunes have waxed and waned until it reached its present boundaries in 1814-15 with the acquisition of the Lombardo-Venetian kingdoms and Dalmatia. The reigning monarch, Francis, declared himself the hereditary emperor of all his states in 1804. These states comprise the archduchy of Austria, the kingdom of Bohemia, the margravate of Moravia, Silesia, the kingdoms of Galicia and Kodomeria, the duchy of Bukovina, Hungary, Transylvania, Dalmatia, Croatia, Sclavonia, Illyria, the Salzsburgh, Tyrol and the Lombardo-Venetian kingdom.

Chief Cities

Capital to many nations, Vienna stands in a fertile plain on the bank of the Danube. It includes many fine buildings and well-built streets and seems to combine the commercial activity of London and the gaiety of Paris with the luxuriance of an eastern city. Prague, the capital of Bohemia, possesses a noble cathedral and a famous university. Cracow, in Galicia, was formerly the capital of Poland. The capital of Hungary is Ofen, or Buda, which is joined to the city of Pest by a bridge of boats.

Population

The total population of about 36,000,000 includes many distinct races, differing widely in manners, language, religion and appearance. One-fifth or so are Germanic in origin, over two-fifths Sclavonic, over one-fifth Romanic and the rest Magyar, Jews and Armenians. The population is very unevenly distributed with about 5,000 to the German square mile in Lombardy, but only 2,000 in Styria (1 German square mile is equal to 22½ English). Mortality is greater than in England or France. Of the whole population most are Roman Catholics, with the highest concentration of Protestants in Hungary. There is no exclusion from any position in the army, law or government by reason of religion. Education is being extensively diffused. The Hungarian and Polish peoples are the least, the Austrians and Lombardo-Venetians the best instructed.

Trade and Industry

The Austrian dominions are rich in their animal, vegetable and mineral productions. They possess some fine breeds of horses, cattle, sheep and goats, cultivate all kinds of grain, fruit, wood and tobacco. The wine produced in Hungary alone amounts to 582,360,000 quarts annually. Two-thirds of exports are received by the adjoining countries, and one third goes by sea, principally from Trieste, Venice and Fiume. The value of imports exceeds that of exports by about one million pounds.

HUNGARY.
SCALE
Miles
HUNGARIAN PEASANTS.
PESTH.
AND THE FORTRESS OF BUDA.
HUNGARIAN NOBLES.
ON THE DANUBE
Longitude East from Greenwich
Krapack or Carpathian Mountains
Eastern Carpathian Mountains
HUNGARY
TRANSYLVANIA
BANAT
SCLAVONIA
CROATIA
TURKEY IN EUROPE
AUSTRIA
ADRIATIC SEA
R. Danube
VIENNA
PESTH
Neusiedler See
Platten See
Grosswardein
Debreczin
Szegedin
Kronstadt
Hermanstadt
Klausenburg
Temesvar
Peterwardein
Belgrade
Semlin
Agram
Carlstadt
Widin

Hungary

AREA AND PHYSICAL ASPECTS

The Hungarian States consist of the ancient kingdom of Hungary, with the provinces of Slavonia and Croatia, the principality of Transylvania and the kingdom of Dalmatia, which together constitute a total area of about 124,000 square miles. While the country is mountainous in the north, west and east, the vast central plain stretches from Vienna to Belgrade with scarcely an eminence. From these fertile plains, the land rises by levels, wooded, sub-alpine and superior alpine. Most of the rivers are tributaries of the great Danube. Of these the Theiss is the largest and follows a winding course for 350 miles. The richest area is the banat or duchy of Temesvar, south-west of Transylvania, which is rich in gold, silver and copper. Precious metals have been mined for 1000 years. The Hungarian opal is also highly esteemed by eastern nations.

HISTORY

The aboriginal races who anciently inhabited the area were conquered first by the Romans, and then by the Huns. About the end of the ninth century a tribe from the Caucasus called the Magyars invaded across the Carpathians and reduced the inhabitants to slavery. In 973 AD their devastating progress was arrested when their leader, Geysa, embraced Christianity. His son Stephen was made hereditary monarch and divided the land into 72 counties. In 1699 the kingdom of Hungary was attached as a fief to the Austrian empire. In an attempt to win their freedom the Hungarians fought a fierce war in 1848-9 but were defeated, and remain subject to Austria, whose emperor presides over the diet, or parliament, as king of Hungary.

POPULATION

The population of the Hungarian States numbers in all over 14,000,000, of whom most are Magyars and Slowacks, although there are sizeable minorities of other races, including Wallachians, Servians, Croats and Germans. The land of the Magyar is therefore a Babel, whose many conflicting interests, diverse languages and adverse feelings prevent all unity of purpose. Most of the Slavonic peoples profess the religion of the Greek church and pray openly for the emperor of Russia, while in Hungary itself there are many Lutherans and Calvinists. Education is in the process of extension, with each nation and religious group having its own schools and colleges, although how far the recent insurrection may have disturbed this state of affairs it is impossible to say.

TRADE AND INDUSTRY

Commerce is small, owing to bad roads, onerous import taxes and vexatious fiscal regulations. There are four great annual fairs held at Pesth, the centre of trade. Black cattle and hogs are extensively exported. The quantity of Tokay wine made annually averages between 80,000 and 100,000 casks, each of fourteen gallons. Some of this wine is kept for a century and then sells for four guineas a bottle. There are several other good wines produced, and altogether about 1,000,000 acres are under the vine. The total quantity of land cultivated in Hungary alone is about the area of England and Wales.

The Illustrations by J. Salmon, & Engraved by S. Fisher.

The Map Drawn & Engraved by J. Rapkin

Prussia

Area and Physical Aspect

Prussia is separated by Hanover and other states into two parts. Rhinish Prussia in the west is the smaller, while the eastern section stretches some 550 miles to the Russian and Polish borders in the east. The whole country is divided into eleven districts. Most of the eastern section forms a great plain, although the south-west of Silesia is mountainous and has a peak 4,724 ft high in the Schnecberg ridge. The Baltic coast provides several good harbours at Dantzic, Memel, Koenigsburg and Swinemunde, and the whole country is scattered with over 1,000 inland lakes. Canals linking the chief rivers form an inland navigation of 700 miles in length. Two islands in the Baltic, Rugen and Bornholm, and various small detached districts in Saxony also belong to Prussia.

History

The Pruzzi, or Sclavonic savages, who migrated to and colonized this area, are represented as being a very primitive people, living in caves or holes in the ground, eating raw flesh and worshipping the snake. They were finally subdued and converted to Christianity by the Teutonic knights in the twelfth century. It was Frederick the Great, king from 1740 to 1786, who raised Prussia to its present position among the European states. The present sovereign ascended the throne in 1840 and has given to his people a free constitution. The national assembly is elected by universal male suffrage.

Chief Cities

Berlin, the capital (population 400,000), is a straggling city on the River Spree, composed of 5 towns. Now 12 miles in circumference, it is defended by a wall and entered by 15 gates. The royal palace is one of the richest dwellings in Europe (see map). Breslau (population 80,000) is the capital and commercial centre of Silesia. Dantzick (population 65,000) is a strong fortification as well as a commercial city with magnificent public edifices. Among other large cities are Dusseldorf, centre of an area of iron manufactories, Cologne, a fine old city with a noble gothic cathedral, and Konisberg, capital of East Prussia.

Population

The kingdom contains about 15,000,000 inhabitants and is in some places more densely populated than any part of England. More than two-thirds are German and the population is rapidly increasing in the fertile districts. There are six universities and schools in very village. 2½ per cent of the state revenue is devoted to public education. Most Prussians are Protestant, but there is perfect toleration of the Roman Catholics.

Trade and Industry

Commerce is active, particularly inland, where there are numerous railways and inland waterways. Silesian linen is valued at £1,500,000 a year. Iron and coal production is high and Berlin china is considered the finest in Europe.

Defence

There is a standing army of 166,000, in which the artillery is reputed to be one of the most efficient in Europe. In addition a *landwehr,* or militia, of 160,000 men assemble yearly for exercise and every man from 20 to 25 is bound to serve.

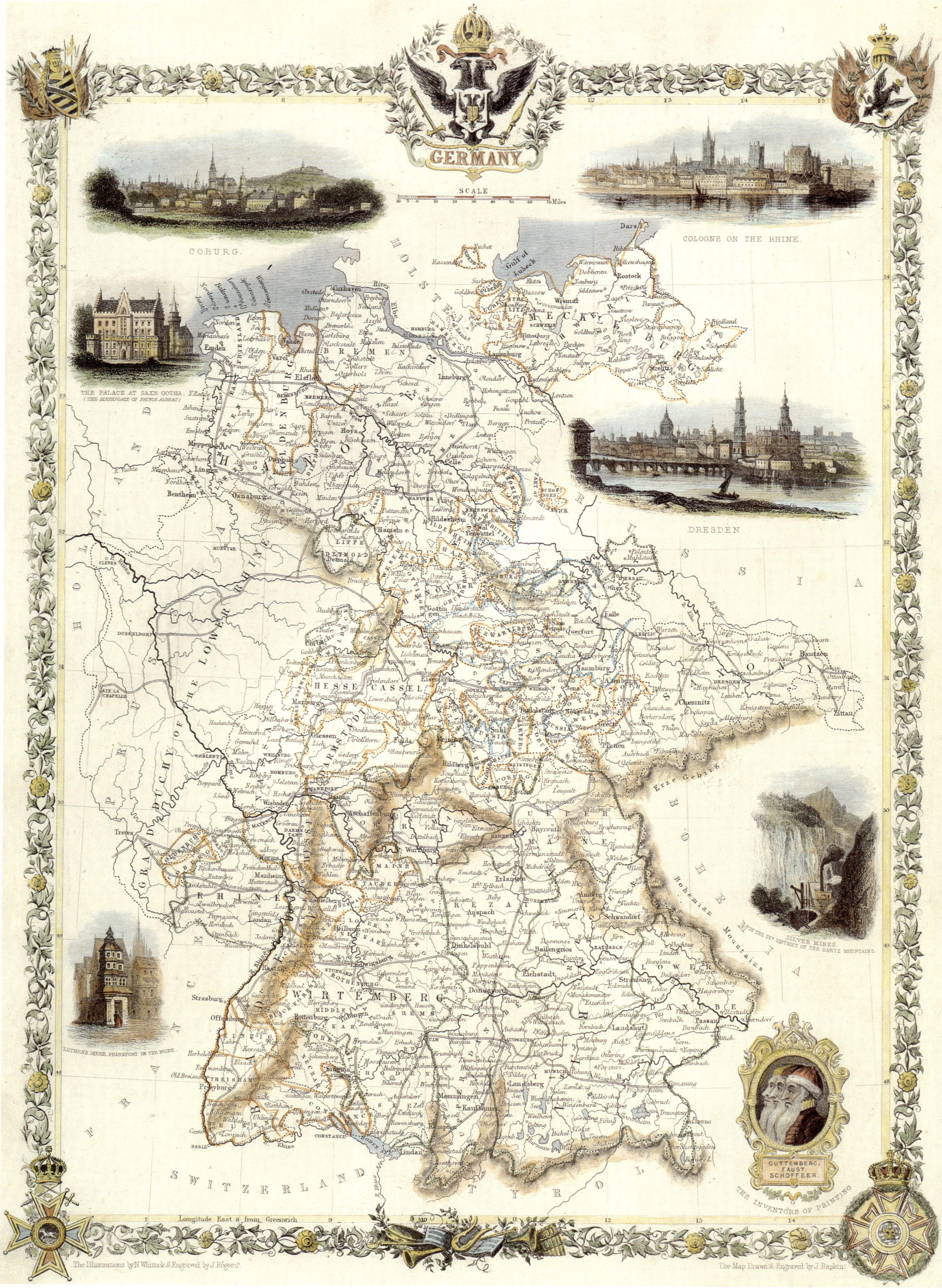
GERMANY
SCALE
Miles
COBURG
COLOGNE ON THE RHINE
THE PALACE AT SAXE GOTHA
DRESDEN
SILVER MINES
LUTHER'S HOUSE, FRANKFORT ON THE MAINE
GUTTEMBERG, FAUST, SCHOFFEER.
THE INVENTORS OF PRINTING
SWITZERLAND
TYROL
BOHEMIA
PRUSSIA
HOLLAND
FRANCE
HOLSTEIN
MECKLENBURG
HANOVER
HESSE CASSEL
WIRTEMBERG
Bohemian Mountains
Longitude East 8 from Greenwich
The Illustrations by H. Warren & Engraved by J. Rogers.
The Map Drawn & Engraved by J. Rapkin.

Germany

The present confederation of German states was formed at the Congress of Vienna at the end of the European War in 1814-15 and consists of 15 larger and 18 smaller independent countries with a total population of 40 million.

BAVARIA is the largest and most populous. Generally flat, although bordered by mountains to the east and south, it has many rivers and lakes, and large areas of forest. Agriculture is extensive. Nearly all the 4,500,000 inhabitants are German and most of these are Roman Catholics. There are schools in every parish and several universities. Munich, the capital, is a handsome city with the finest gallery of rare pictures in Europe. Government is by a hereditary sovereign and a national assembly.

WIRTEMBERG, west of Bavaria, is partly mountainous, but mainly champagne lands and well watered plains. There are silver, copper, coal and iron mines. Cherries are grown here to make the liquor *kirschwasser*, and millions of snails are fattened in autumn and sent to Vienna and Italy. The population numbers 1,800,000 of whom most are Lutherans. Education is probably the most extensive in Europe, with every child between 6 and 14 being required to attend school by law. The capital, Stuttgard has a magnificent palace. A constitutional monarchy.

BADEN was created a state in the twelfth century and is chiefly hilly country with beautiful scenery and a healthy climate. There are 300 hot mineral springs, much resorted to for bathing. In the principal mountain range of Suabia, the Schwarz Wold (highest point 4,300 feet), the Danube has its source. Of the 1,400,000 inhabitants, most are Roman Catholics. There are schools of industry in every village and commerce is mostly in manufactured goods, such as arms, and hardware, paper, and wooden clocks. A hereditary principality in the male line with two houses of legislature, the upper chosen by the grand duke and other nobility, the lower by all males over 25.

SAXONY is mountainous towards the south and level in the north. There are many rivers flowing through the beautiful valleys and abundant mineral wealth. Silver, tin, bismuth, manganese, copper, etc. are mined and porcelain clay and marble are also to be found. Most of the 1,900,000 inhabitants are Roman Catholics. The country is divided into five provinces, with the capital at Dresden, famed for its manufactures and annual fairs, especially that for the sale of books. There is extensive manufacture of cloth in Saxony, with 250 mills and 20,000 machines for stockings alone. Government is by an hereditary monarchy.

HANOVER was raised from an electorate to a kingdom in 1815 and the sovereignty of the country has been held by the kings of England since 1714. An immense plain of heath and sandhills with some minerals in the Harz mountains along the south-west frontier. The population numbers 1,800,000 mostly Lutheran. The capital is Hanover, an antique-looking town on the river Leine.

The smaller states include Mecklenburg, Hesse, Darmstadt, Nassau, and Coburg and Gotha, the birth-place of the illustrious consort of our beloved sovereign.

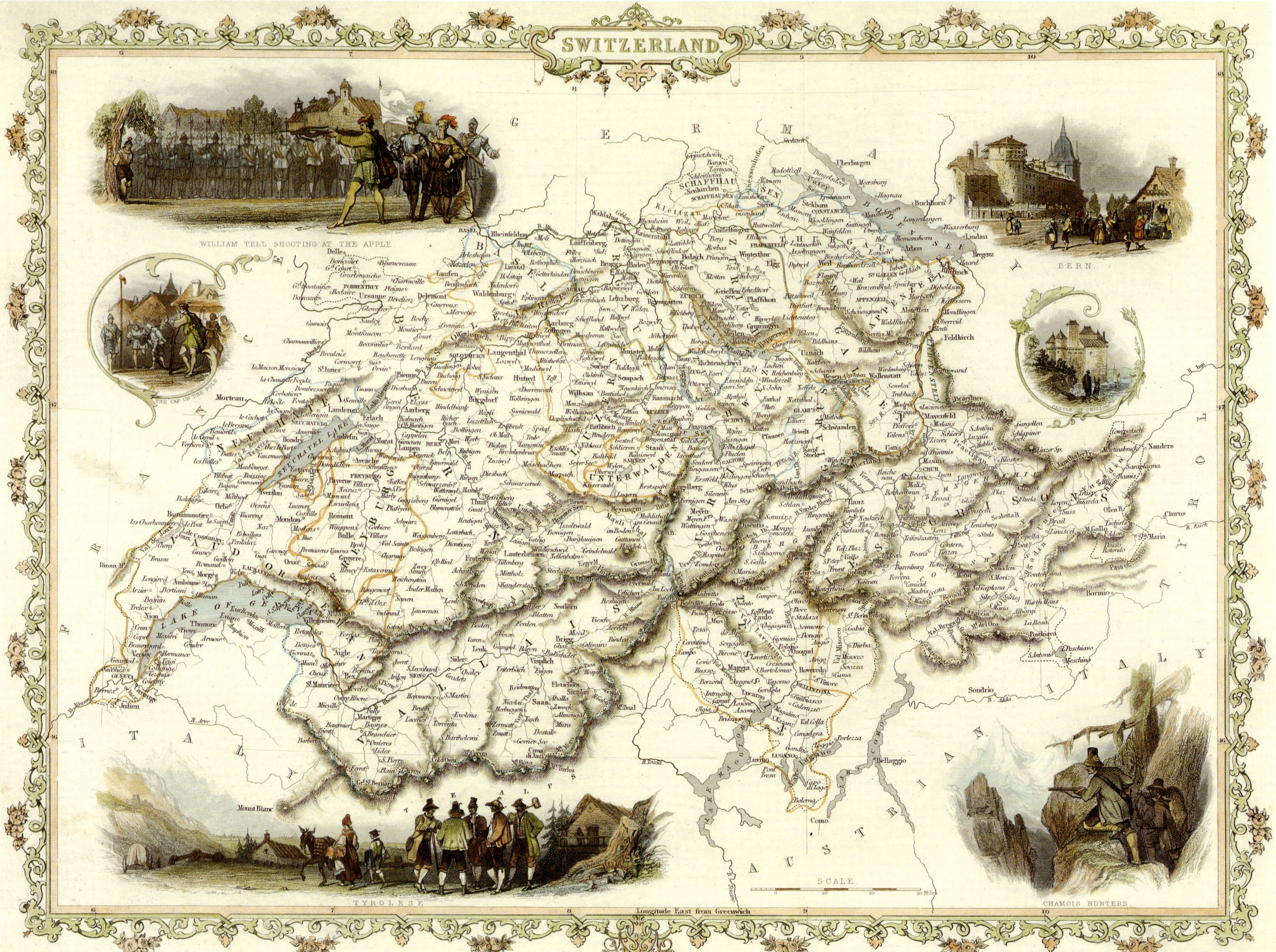

The Illustrations by A.H. Wray, & Engraved by J.B. Allen.
The Map Drawn & Engraved by J. Rapkin

Switzerland

AREA AND PHYSICAL ASPECT

The Swiss Confederacy consists of 22 independent cantons and has been variously estimated at from 15,000 to nearly 19,000 British square miles in area. The most mountainous region in Europe, with the highest alps reaching up to 15,000 feet above the sea and many peaks always covered in snow. The glaciers present a scene of desolation where only the thundering crash of great icebergs and avalanches can be heard. Between the mountains are verdant valleys with rich corn fields and picturesque villages.

RIVERS AND LAKES

The Rhine flows 200 miles along the borders of Switzerland and forms a celebrated cataract after Schaffhausen. The Rhône rises from a glacier in the Valais and is fed by several smaller streams before entering Lake Geneva. There are many lakes, chief of which are Geneva, or Leman, 330 English square miles in area and in some places 1,000 feet deep; Constance, over 1,000 feet above the sea, through which the Rhine passes; Lugano, Luzern, Zurich and Neufchatel.

CLIMATE

Cold in the mountains, temperate in the plains and hot in summer in the southern valleys. The lower limit of perpetual snow is 9,000 feet, and the upper limit for the growth of trees is 1,400 feet. There are several remarkable native animals, including the ibex, chamois and marmot. Fish are plentiful in the lakes.

HISTORY

Named Helvetia by the Romans who conquered it under Julius Caesar, various parts of the country were later annexed by the Germans, Burgundians and French. In the fourteenthth century the Swiss began a gallant struggle for independence which lasted for nearly two hundred years. When the doctrines of the Reformation were introduced in the sixteenth century, civil war broke out between the Protestant and Roman Catholic cantons. The confederation was finally recognized as an independent state in 1648, and perpetual neutrality granted in 1815.

POPULATION

Now 2,000,000 in total, about two-thirds speak German, 100,000 Italian, 50,000 Romanish and the remainder French. There is much jealousy between the cantons, though a common danger would probably unite them. Most belong to the reformed church, which is Presbyterian. Education is extensive in the Protestant cantons but neglected in other districts.

TRADE AND INDUSTRY

Commerce is limited, but manufactures are increasing and in many valleys steam-engines and mills are at work preparing imported cotton. In Geneva the manufacture of watches and jewellery is carried to great perfection. Swiss cloth and leather goods are esteemed for their durability.

GOVERNMENT

The Confederacy which unites the cantons has lasted five centuries. The National Diet or Parliament sits annually and alternately at Zurich, Berne and Luzern, the chief magistrate of the host canton being president for that year. Each canton also has its own local government, some of democratic constitution, others more aristocratic in form, with which the Diet does not interfere.

NORTHERN ITALY.
SWITZERLAND
TYROL
FRANCE
SARDINIAN STATES
LOMBARDY
VENETIAN
TUSCANY
NAPLES
ADRIATIC SEA OR GULF OF VENICE
MEDITERRANEAN SEA
GULF OF GENOA
GULF OF GAETA
STRAIT OF BONIFACIO
THE GRAND CANAL, VENICE.
S.T PETER'S, ROME.
SCALE
Longitude East 8 from Greenwich
The Illustrations by A.H. Wray, & Engraved by J.B. Allen.
The Map Drawn & Engraved by J. Rapkin.

Northern Italy

Area and Physical Aspect

Italy, the most favoured portion of Europe in respect to position, climate, scenery and soil is sheltered to the north by the Alps and bathed by the Adriatic and Mediterranean Seas. The accompanying map includes the northern portion as far south as the Papal States. The countries included here are the kingdom of Sardinia (including the Sardinian States and the island of Sardinia), Venetian-Lombardy, the duchies of Parma, Modena, Massa Carrara, Lucca, San Marino and Tuscany, and the Papal States. The natural features of the country are as varied as the political divisions. The Alps slope down to the shores of the Mediterranean, except for the Apennines which pass down the centre of Italy, separating Tuscany from the other states. Mont Blanc is the highest peak, at 15,200 feet. The principal river is the Po, with a course of 300 miles, which is navigable after Turin. The Tiber is 150 miles long, and 300 feet wide at Rome.

History

After the collapse of the Roman Empire the Ostrogoths spread themselves over Italy and formed a new empire extending from Sicily to the Danube, of which Verona was made the capital. Further invasions followed, first by the Greeks, then by the Lombards and finally by the Franks under Charlemagne. He bestowed part of the country on Pope Leo III. The state of Savoy increased from a small county in 1016, through marriages and wars into a kingdom. Venice, after thirteen centuries of independence, was given to the Austrians in 1805. The duchy of Modena is now in the possession of the house of Este; the duchy of Parma belongs to the duchess of Lucca, Napoleon's sister, who was also made grand duchess of Tuscany, though this last has since reverted to Austria. The Papal States, having remained in the hands of the popes more or less uninterruptedly since 774, became a republic in 1848, when Pius IX fled in disguise.

Chief Cities

There are a greater number of noble and classical cities in Italy than to be found within the same area in any other country. Rome, Milan, Venice, Florence, Genoa, Turin, Parma, Lucca, all attest the former opulence, art and industry of the Italians. Rome is generally acknowledged the most beautiful, and contains magnificent palaces filled with the treasures of ancient and modern art in addition to the Vatican, the marble-covered church of St Peter and stupendous ruins.

Population

With a total population of 14,971,549, this part of Italy has remained strongly Roman Catholic throughout the centuries. The dialects spoken in the several districts differ greatly. Education among the lower classes is neglected and even the universities are ill-managed. The separate states are isolated, each having their own government, but all more or less subject to Austria.

Trade and Industry

Exports are small, consisting chiefly of silk, rice, fruit, oil and musical instruments. The maritime commerce, which once powerfully influenced Europe and Asia, particularly at the height of the Venetian Republic and of Genoese trade, is now scarcely worth noticing.

SOUTHERN ITALY.
PAPAL STATES
GULF OF VENICE
GULF OF MANFREDONIA
GULF OF TARANTO
GULF OF SQUILLACE
GULF OF EUPHEMIA
GULF OF GIOIA
STRAIT OF MESSINA
STRAIT OF BONIFACIO
GULF OF SALERNO
BAY OF NAPLES
GULF OF GAETA
GULF OF CAGLIARI
ÆOLIAN OR LIPARI ISLANDS
SICILY
SARDINIA
CORSICA
MEDITERRANEAN
AFRICA
IONIAN SEA
THE CARNIVAL.
BENEVENTO.
NAPLES AND VESUVIUS.
FESTIVAL OF THE VINTAGE.
SCALE.
Miles.
Longitude East from Greenwich

Southern Italy

Area and Physical Aspect

The map of Southern Italy contains the kingdom of Naples and the island of Sicily, or as they are commonly known, the Two Sicilies. The area of the continental territory is estimated at 31,040 square miles, that of the island about 11,300 square miles. Sicily appears to have been first separated from Naples by some convulsion of the earth and gradually isolated by encroachments of the sea which have formed the Straits of Messina (five miles broad). The ridge of the Apennines passes through both from north to south along the mainland and then from east to west through Sicily. There are several volcanoes in the region, many of them still active, including Vesuvius near Naples, Etna in Sicily, and Stromboli on one of the Aeolian or Lipari islands. Mount Maccaluba in Sicily ejects cold mud and clay, accompanied by a subterranean noise, and there is also a wind volcano in Sicily, the Dinnamare. The bays are numerous and considerable. All the mainland rivers descend from the Apennines and have consequently but a short course.

Climate

The warmest in Europe. The Sirocco, or African wind, often prevails and destroys vegetation.

History

Originally colonized by some Grecian tribes, the whole area fell into Roman hands in 481 BC After the fall of the Roman Empire the histories of Naples and Sicily remained separate until Charles V inherited both crowns and they became a Spanish province for two centuries. Given independence in 1759 the kingdom of Naples is now an hereditary monarchy with a representative assembly. It is divided into twelve mainland provinces, and three on Sicily.

Chief Cities

The capital of Southern Italy is Naples, which is built in a semi-circular form along the Bay of Naples. The wealthiest and best populated city in all Italy, it contains 300 churches, and the cathedral is dedicated to St Januarius, patron saint of the city. Naples' chief drawback is its vicinity to Vesuvius. Capua, a fine town, is in a country abounding with natural steam baths and sulphurous lakes. Palermo, the capital of Sicily (population 180,000), stands on a small bay at the end of a kind of natural amphitheatre. Messina, which stands on the Strait of that name, is the most important commercial town in the kingdom and possesses a harbour which could contain 4,000 ships. The inhabitants are still repairing the ravages of the earthquake in 1783. Syracuse has some remarkable antiquities. Catania (population 45,000) was founded seven centuries BC and has spacious streets paved with lava.

Population

The total number of people is 7,500,000, of which 2,000,000 are Sicilians. The religion is Roman Catholic, and the king, as Beatissimo Padre, is head of the church. There are three universities, at Naples, Palermo and Catania, but few means of public instruction for the poor.

Commerce and Industry

The chief produce of the region is agricultural. There are many olive and citrus fruit groves, and an abundance of grain, wine and silk.

SWEDEN AND NORWAY.
STOCKHOLM.
SCALE.
120 Miles.
NORWEGIAN PEASANTRY.
NORWEGIAN LAPLANDERS. (WINTER DRESS)
IRON MINE OF DANNEMORA, UPSALA.
NORWEGIAN SKIELOBERE OR SKATE RUNNERS.
PEASANTS OF SWEDEN.
ATLANTIC OCEAN
GULF OF BOTHNIA
GULF OF FINLAND
GULF OF RIGA
BALTIC SEA
SKAGER RACK
CATTEGAT
Arctic Circle
LOFFODEN ISLES
TROMSEN ISLES
FINMARK
LAPLAND
TORNEA LAPPMARK
LULEA LAPPMARK
PITEA LAPPMARK
UMEA LAPPMARK
ANGERMANLAND
HELSINGLAND
CHRISTIANIA
STOCKHOLM
COPENHAGEN
CHRISTIANSTAD
CARLSKRONA
North Cape
Hammerfest
Tromsoe
Tornea
Uleaborg
Umea
Trondhiem
Christiansund
Bergen
Stavanger
Gottenburg
Upsala
Gefle
Nykoping
Kalmar
Wisby
Gotland
Oeland
Bornholm I.
Aland Is.
Abo
Borgo
Revel
Dago I.
Oesel I.
Riga
Libau
Memel
Aalborg
The Skaw
Varanger Fiord
Longitude East 14 from Greenwich

Sweden and Norway

These kingdoms have been united under the rule of the same sovereign since 1814, although they retain distinct constitutions and administrations.

Area and Physical Aspects

Together Sweden and Norway cover an area of 323,360 square miles. They are separated by a ridge of mountains varying from 3,000 to 6,000 feet in height and 1,000 miles in length. The Atlantic strikes with considerable force on the Norwegian coast and has caused the formation of many islands and extensive fiords. The celebrated whirlpool of Malstrom on the north coast is about two miles wide and probably communicates with a subterranean passage through which the sea finds its way into the Gulf of Bothnia. The scenery in both countries is wild and grand the mountains thickly clad with pine forests, the waters remarkably clear. There are innumerable lakes, some of large size. Wenern in south Sweden is 100 miles long and is united to Wettern, also 100 miles long, and Malar, the lake on which Stockholm is built, by the Gotha Canal which affords a passage for vessels from the Baltic to the North Sea between April and November.

Climate

In the south the climate is similar to that of north-eastern England, but the northern winters are very severe and during the winter solstice the sun does not appear above the horizon for weeks. The splendid Aurora borealis, or northern lights, in some degree compensates for these long nights; and in the summer the sun does not set completely for two and a half months.

Chief Cities

Stockholm, the capital of Sweden, is favourably situated for trade on an inlet of the Baltic. Bergen, the capital of Norway, is a harbour on the Atlantic coast, where most buildings are constructed of wood.

History

Sweden, originally peopled by the Finns and Lapponians, was reduced to regular government in 954 AD by Olof, one of the Upsala kings who embraced Christianity. Queen Margaret of Denmark united Sweden and Norway to her dominions in 1397. But in 1448 they separated from Denmark and chose their own king. In 1810 on the death of the prince royal, the Swedish states elected the French marshal Bernadotte as their sovereign. He obtained Norway in 1814, and his son, Francis Gustavus Oscar, is now king of Sweden and Norway. Both countries have a parliament of two houses, in which the four orders of nobles, clergy, burghers and peasants are represented.

Population

Sweden has about 3,100,000 inhabitants, Norway 1,200,000. Most are Lutherans and, although only about 3 acres of land in 50 are cultivated there are few paupers. The peoples of both countries are of Germano-Celtic origin and their languages, although different, have many points of resemblance.

Trade and Industry

Sweden abounds in iron, which is esteemed the finest in the world. There are also copper, gold, silver and lead mines. Many thousands of pounds of minerals are exported from both countries every year, as are thousands of lasts of timber. Duties levied on foreign goods are comparatively high in both countries and some British goods are prohibited.

DENMARK
COPENHAGEN
SKAGER RACK
CATTEGAT
SWEDEN
NORTH SEA
BALTIC SEA
THE SOUND
LAHOLM BAY
KIOGE BAY
The Skawe
Gottenburg
Warberg
Falkenberg
Halmstad
Helsingborg
Elsinore
Landskrona
Malmo
LÆSSOE
Anholdt
SAMSOE
FIORD
Aalborg
Horsens
Fredericia
Kolding
Helgoland
SYLTOE
FORA
FEHMERN
Kiel
Lubeck
Wismar
Rostock
Stralsund
Cuxhaven
Altona
Harburg
HANOVER
PRUSSIA
MECKLENBURG
ELSINORE
SLESWIG
SCALE
Longitude East from Greenwich

Denmark

Area and Physical Aspect

This ancient kingdom now consists of the Danish islands in the Baltic, the Jutland peninsula, the duchies of Sleswig, Holstein and Lauenberg, Iceland and the Feroe islands. Denmark is a great plain, the highest eminence being only 1,200 feet above the sea. Although northern Jutland is bleak and barren, the rest of the country is well cultivated and productive. Rivers and lakes are small. The Baltic and North Seas are connected by the Kieler Canal in north Sleswig. Iceland, an island in the Atlantic close to the Arctic Circle, is a country of volcanic mountains (some 6,000 feet in height), boiling fountains, barren plains, and scattered fertile valleys. The hot springs or geysers are extraordinary, clouds of steam and boiling water being thrown up to 90 feet in the air from pits of pipes in the ground. There are 25 Feroe Islands, 17 inhabited, which rise up to 3,000 feet from the sea between the Shetland Isles and Iceland.

Climate

The great extent of sea and the flat coast render the air humid and foggy. Winter cold can be severe and summer heat oppressive. Generally, however, the climate is salubrious, as attested by the abundant agricultural produce and the fine herds of horses for which Denmark, and especially Holstein, is famous.

History

Denmark and the other Scandinavian countries were probably peopled by migrating hordes who passed from the north to warmer climates. The first king of Denmark is said to have been Skiold, son of Odin, leader of the Goths. Under the name Northmen or Normans they swept along the coasts of Europe, even reaching as far as Constantinople. In 1397 the Danish princess Margaret joined the crowns of Denmark, Norway and Sweden in a union that lasted 150 years. There have been frequent wars between Denmark and Sweden, although the two countries are now at peace. Denmark is a hereditary monarchy with a representative assembly and a privy council. Sleswig, Holstein and Lauenberg have separate governors and their own provincial laws. Iceland is divided into four provinces, and a *stiftamtamn*, or ruler, is appointed by the king of Denmark every five years. Denmark also has small colonies in the West Indies, on the west coast of Africa and in the Bay of Bengal.

Chief Cities

Copenhagen (population 100,000) has been capital of the Danish dominions since 1443. Situated on the east coast of the island of Zealand, it is a noble-looking, well-fortified city, five miles in circumference. Next in size is Altona, upon the Elbe near Hamburg, a commercial port of about 35,000.

Population

Denmark has about 2,000,000 inhabitants, Iceland about 60,000. Both countries are Lutheran in religion. Every Danish town or village has a primary school and there are many higher educationary establishments. The Icelanders, too, are well educated, many speaking and writing Latin as well as Danish.

Trade and Industry

Foreign and coasting trade is active. Corn is grown and cattle, horses and sheep bred. Iceland produces sulphur, alum and various volcanic materials. The Feroe islanders are mainly fishermen and bird-catchers.

HOLLAND
SCALE
ROTTERDAM
ON THE DORT
DUTCH PEASANTS
Longitude East from Greenwich

Holland

Area and Physical Aspect

This region of rivers, lakes and canals, whose surface is for a large part beneath the level of the ocean, is a remarkable illustration of what may be accomplished by a brave, enterprising and industrious people. Slightly elevated in the eastern districts, the rest of the country is flat. The north and west areas below sea level are kept dry by vast artificial dykes partly protected by sand hillocks. These are usually 30 feet high and 70 feet broad at the base, made of rough clay and fenced. In violent storms dykes may be covered with sail cloth to mitigate the force of the sea since the inundations caused by breaches cause much destruction of life and property. The Zuydersee, 1207 square miles in area, is supposed to have been originally a fresh-water lake. There are numerous canals, the Dutch ship canal connecting Amsterdam with the harbour of Niewediep being the greatest work of the kind in Europe, which cost £1,000,000 to build and was finished in 1825. The rivers Rhine, Scheldt and Maese flow through Holland. The country is cultivated with skill, and covered with neat towns and handsome villas.

History

Known to the Romans as Belgic Gaul, the area of Holland was divided into two by the Franks. Over the centuries it passed from German, to Burgundian and in the sixteenth century to Spanish hands. After a strenuous struggle for freedom, supported by the Prince of Orange, independence was finally granted in 1648. From that time the Dutch made great progress in navigation and commerce, and it is said that 2,000 vessels a year were being built in their ports. Maritime rivalry provoked lengthy wars with England and Dutch colonies were gradually reduced. They now own Java and parts of the Eastern Archipelago. Belgium separated itself from Holland by a revolution in 1830. The population was estimated in 1842 at 3,100,000. Government is by a hereditary sovereign and two legislative chambers.

Chief Cities

Amsterdam (population 202,364) and Rotterdam (72,294) are the two main ports for foreign trade, and Amsterdam is one of the finest cities in Europe, being built on piles and intersected by canals. The Hague, Leyden, Haarlem and other places also attest the wealth and industry of the Dutch.

Trade and Industry

42 per cent of Dutch trade is with Britain; the number of English vessels entering Dutch ports in 1840 was 2,196. The chief products are agricultural and come from the dairies and orchards. Grain, potatoes and tobacco are also grown in quantity. Fishery has declined. At one time there are said to have been 9,000 boats manned by 50,000 men engaged in the herring trade, but the corresponding figures for 1842 were 1,605 boats and 8,350 men.

Revenue

Including the municipal duties on articles of drink, food and fuel, there is no country so highly taxed as Holland. The revenue for 1842 was 71,103,451 florins, or nearly six million pounds sterling. Even so, the country has a large national debt of £170,000,000.

BELGIUM.
UNION FAIT LA FORCE
NORTH SEA
HOLLAND
ANTWERP
FLANDERS
SOUTH BRABANT
HAINAULT
NAMUR
LIEGE
LUXEMBOURG
PRUSSIA
FRANCE
ANTWERP CATHEDRAL
ALTAR OF ST GUDULE, BRUSSELS.
MONUMENTS ON THE PLAINS OF WATERLOO.
SCALE.
Miles.
Longitude East from Greenwich.
The Illustrations by J. Marchant & Engraved by J. B. Allen.
The Map Drawn & Engraved by J. Rapkin.

Belgium

Area and Physical Aspect

With an area of 12,569 square miles, Belgium is flat for the greater part, rising in gradual elevations towards the south and east. In Luxembourg a branch of the Ardennes mountains and large forests impart a bold and romantic character to the country. In the provinces of Flanders and Antwerp the vast unbroken plain is covered with the most luxuriant cultivation presenting more the appearance of gardens than of fields. Belgium is well watered. The Meuse, Maas, or Maese, which rises in France and falls into the Rhine, is navigable throughout the whole of its course in Belgium.

History

According to tradition, the early inhabitants, named Firl-bogs, invaded Ireland in 2503 BC. Thereafter linked with Holland, under the Roman name Gallia Belgica and later as the Low Countries, Belgian history followed the same course as the Dutch, being occupied successively by Franks, Burgundians and Spanish. In 1794 the French occupied and retained the territory but it was restored to Holland in 1814. In 1830, after some fighting the Belgians succeeded in gaining their independence and in 1841 they elected as their king prince Leopold of Saxe Coburg. The country is now divided into 9 provinces and is a limited monarchy with legislative power vested in the king and in two chambers, the senate and the house of representatives. The qualification for voting is the annual payment of direct taxes to the amount of 35*s*.

Chief Cities

Brussels, the capital, is built on hills and has a commanding appearance. Continuous streets, extensive suburbs and fine gardens combine to render the city a miniature Paris. The Hotel de Ville is one of the most imposing municipal structures in Europe. South of Brussels, the field of Waterloo is a well-cultivated plain on which a huge mound has been formed to commemorate the terrific battle of 1815 which decided the fate of Napoleon. Antwerp, once a much larger city than now, has the finest gothic cathedral in Europe with walls and paintings by Reubens. Bruges, the ancient capital of the Low Countries, is still a perfect specimen of a medieval town.

Population

Distinct from the peoples of France and Holland, the Belgians possess some of the characteristics of both nations. The total population is over 4,000,000, of whom most are Roman Catholics. Education is extensive in primary branches.

Trade and Industry

Agriculture is the staple of the country, with 2,120,342 acres given over to grain. Flax is a most profitable crop, bringing in as much as £220 a ton. In addition there are 40 mines in the country, and 3 to 4 million tons of coal and 328,000 tons of iron are raised annually. The great iron works at Seraing is the largest establishment of the kind in Europe and employs from two to three thousand artisans. There are extensive manufactories for the casting of cannon and the making of fire-arms of which there is a large export. Exports to Britain are valued at 15,289,072 francs, nearly twice those of imports from the same country.

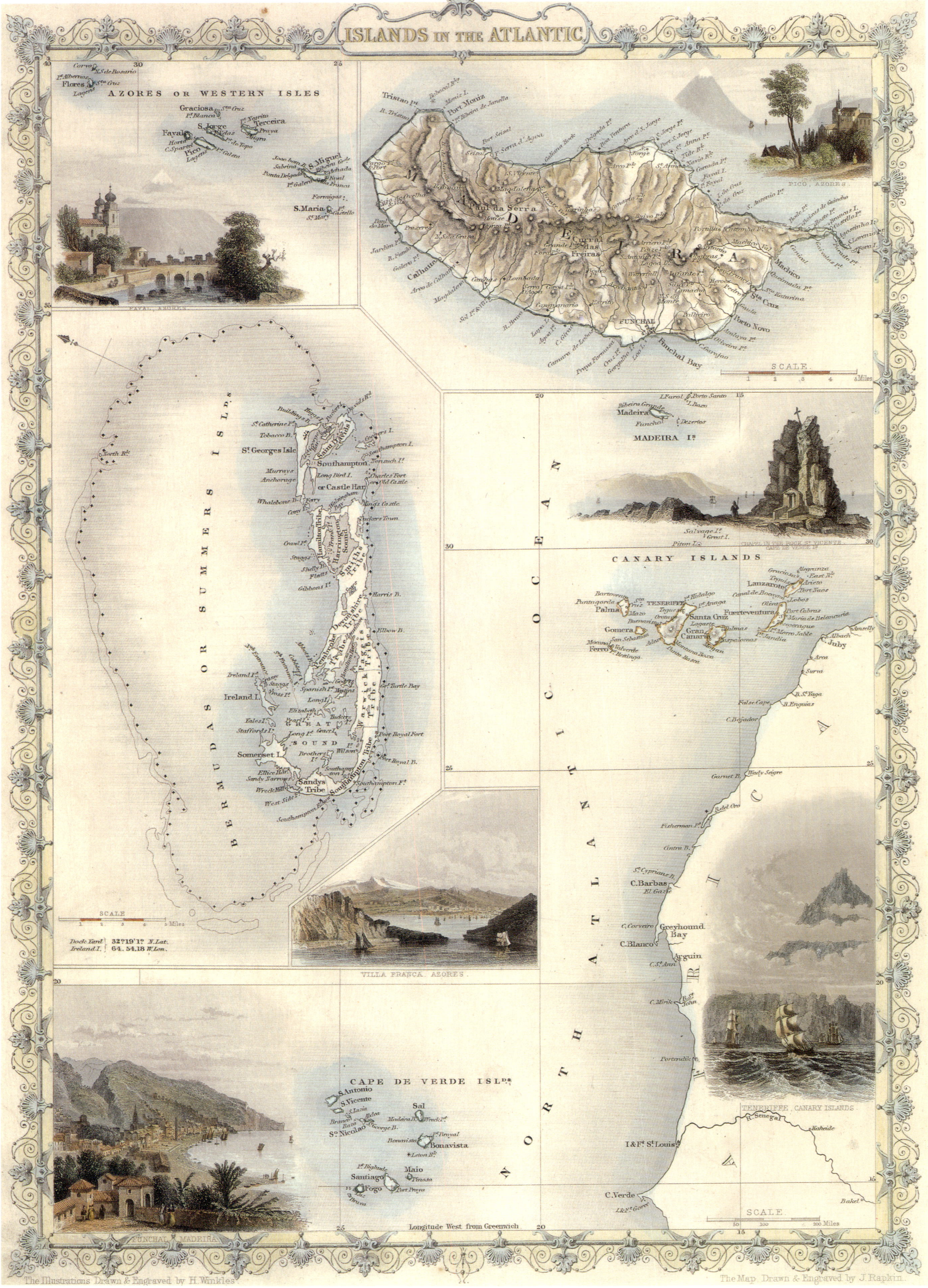

The Illustrations Drawn & Engraved by H. Winkles.

The Map Drawn & Engraved by J. Rapkin.

Islands in the Atlantic

The groups delineated in the accompanying map are the Bermudas, Madeira, Canary, Azores and Cape Verde Islands.

THE BERMUDAS, or Somer Isles, exceeding 300 in number, lie about 600 miles east of South Carolina and contain about 12,000 acres. They were discovered in 1522 by Bermudez, a Spaniard, and settled in the 17th century from Virgina and England, remaining in the uninterrupted possession of England. In comparison to many of the West Indies they are low, the highest point not exceeding 200 feet. The principal islands lie in such a manner as to form harbours capacious and deep enough for the whole British navy but difficult of access. The island of St George, military station of the colony and formerly the seat of government, lies at the entrance to the only passage for ships of burthen. The most important work is a breakwater, on which several hundred convicts are employed, and the dockyard is kept in fine order. A total population of 8,451 enjoy a climate favourable to European health.

MADEIRA owes its name to the Portuguese who took possession of it in 1419. Lying about 360 miles from the west coast of Africa, the island has an area of 407 square miles. It is decidedly mountainous, with Ruivo peak, the highest point, about 6,000 feet above the sea. The scenery is varied and picturesque and has been much admired by travellers. Funchal, the chief town (population about 15,000) is built around a bay in which anchorage is good, although vessels are exposed to southerly gales. It is the favourite residence of English invalids, or of persons of a consumptive nature who come to take advantage of the equable distribution of temperature throughout the year. Volcanic eruptions have occurred on different occasions. There are a few small detached islands in the same group.

THE CANARY ISLANDS are seven in number and are under Spanish domination. Teneriffe, the largest, is extremely mountainous and has a population of about 100,000. There is a celebrated volcanic cone on the island rising about 2 and a quarter miles above the sea. Santa Cruz is the chief town. Grand Canary, from which the group derives its name, has about 60,000 inhabitants. Comparatively well-cultivated it yields an excellent wine, together with an abundance of various kinds of fruit. The other, smaller islands, are Fuerta Ventura, Palma, Lauzerota, Ferro and Gomera.

THE AZORES or Western Islands were named Ilhos dos Acores (islands of Hawks) when discovered by the Portuguese in l445. Volcanic in origin they lie some 250 miles west of the Portuguese coast and are generally rugged and mountainous with very beautiful scenery. The total population of 208,500 live on nine islands, the most populous being St Miguel, whose principal town, Pont Delgado, is the most flourishing in the Azores.

THE CAPE VERDE ISLANDS are ten in number and belong to the Portuguese. They are generally mountainous. Santiago, the seat of government, contains about 12,000 people among whom there are few white persons.

BRITISH POSSESSIONS IN THE MEDITERRANEAN
GIBRALTAR
GIBRALTAR BAY
NEUTRAL GROUND
MEDITERRANEAN SEA
Catalan Bay & Village
Old Mole
New Mole
Europa Pt.
GOZO
Rabatto
Comino
FREGHI ROAD
Melleha B.
St. Pauls Bay
VALETTA
Grand Harbour
Ft. Ricasoli
Bengemma Hills
CITTA VECCHIA
RABATTO
Zebbug
Zabbar
Marsa Scirocco
Pt. Delimara
CORFU
ALBANIA
CHANNEL OF CORFU
Citadel
Butrinto
Port Papajanni
C. Bianco
S. Mathias
Clomo
Egripo
Anti Paxo
Gavo
VATHI ITHACA
SANTA MAURA
ITHACA
Vathi
CEPHALONIA
ARGOSTOLI
C. Kapri
Gulf of Argostoli
Meganisi
Kalamo
Kastus
Gulf of Patras
Kurzolari
ZANTE
Zante Tn. & Bay
Gulf of Kieri
CERIGO
MOREA

British Possessions in the Mediterranean

GIBRALTAR, a promontory three miles long, forms the southern part of the continent of Europe. The natural strength of the position was probably first noticed in the eighth century when the Moors invaded. They remained in possession of the fortress until 1462. The conquest of Gibraltar by the English was accomplished in 1704 and it has continued in English hands ever since, despite frequent attempts to wrest it from them. The highest point of the craggy ridge which runs north to south along its length is Sugar Loaf Point, 1,439 feet above sea level. The northern point of the peninsula is connected with the mainland. The total number of guns serviceable in the garrison is now more than 1,000. In 1848 the civil population numbered about 12,000, although this figure fluctuates. The inhabitants are of many nations, including English, Spaniards, Moorish, etc. Schools are good and there is an excellent garrison library. The temperature is warm and there are occasional hail storms accompanied by thunder, with coruscations, falling stars and other meteoric phenomena.

ALTA and GOZO are situated between Sicily and the African coast. Known in ancient times as Melita, Malta appears to have been at successive periods in the possession of the Phoenicians, Carthaginians, Greeks, Romans, Arabs, Knights of St John and French. The British have been in occupation since 1800. Formerly placed by all geographers in Africa, but declared by a British Act of Parliament to be in Europe as regards the service of our soldiery, Malta has a circumference of 60 to 70 miles. The hill and dale surface is beautifully diversified and the industrious Maltese have converted an apparently barren rock into very picturesque country. The ports of Valetta and Marsa Sirocco are capable of holding a great number of vessels. Gozo, to the west of Malta, is 20 miles in circumference. Although fertile and thickly inhabited it contains no town, the people being scattered in villages protected by a central fort. The total population of both islands numbers about 120,000.

The IONIAN ISLANDS are situated in the Ionian Sea between the Albanian coast and the southern extremity of the Morean peninsula. After early colonization by the Greeks, they passed into the hands of the Romans, Venetians, Turks and French before coming under British protection in 1815. The seat of government is at Corfu, a mountainous island about 35 miles long from north to south, and 12 miles wide at its broadest. Cephalonia, although second in rank to Corfu, is the largest of the septinsular union. Rugged and mountainous, its highest peak is Black Mountain, 3,625 feet above sea level. Zante, 10 miles distant from Cephalonia, has an area of 156 square miles. From its exquisite beauty it is known by common consent as 'il fiore di Levante', and the city of Zante is very imposing in appearance when viewed from the sea. These three, together with Ithaca, Santa Maura, Paxo, and Cerigo have a total population of about 220,000 whose language and religion is that of the Greeks.

The Illustrations by H. Warren; & Engraved by J. H. Kernot.

The Map, Drawn & Engraved by J. Rapkin.

Overland Route to India

For about 250 years, all mercantile and personal intercourse between Europe, India, and the East has been carried on by the tedious, stormy and often disastrous voyage of 15,000 miles round the southern promontory of Africa. The junction of an Anglo-Indian army from Bombay (via the Red Sea) with British troops from England (via the Mediterranean) under the masterly policy of the late Marquess Wellesley at the commencement of the present century plainly evidenced the practicability of this route of about 7,000 miles. At that time, however, the East India Company possessed a monopoly of the trade with India; a fine fleet of large merchant ships were the sole mediums of transit between Great Britain, India and China; and it was not deemed advisable to take advantage of the Marquess Wellesley's example. however, the extension of our power, the necessity for the early receipt of information from India during long-continued wars and the application of steam to ocean navigation gradually overcame all private interests.

Around 1830, therefore, several gentlemen made great efforts for the establishment of a mail steam communication via the Red Sea. At length a Dublin Steam Packet Company obtained a contract for conveyance of mails from Southampton to Egypt, transit from Cairo to Suez was arranged, and the East India Company placed their armed steamers on the line from Suez to Bombay. Ultimately the Irish company was extended into a 'Peninsular and Oriental' company, and it now conveys the mails, passengers and light goods once a month each way between England, Calcutta and Hong Kong.

At present there are three main routes. The first takes passengers and mails by ship across the Bay of Biscay and the Mediterranean to Alexandria. They are then conveyed up the Nile to Cairo, across the desert in horse-drawn omnibus to Suez, a distance of 86 miles, and thence by ship to Aden, and Ceylon. From here the main steamer proceeds to Calcutta, while smaller vessels continue to Bombay.

By the second route, travellers are taken from London to Paris and Marseille, there embarking on a vessel to Alexandria and finishing the journey as detailed for the first route. The third route, termed the German Overland, returns from Alexandria by steam vessels to Greece and thence up the Adriatic to Trieste. Disembarking, the passenger may travel by diligence or post carriage to Vienna and from there by a combination of train and carriage to Hamburg and finally across the North Sea to the river Thames or to Ostend and across the English Channel.

Another route, on the high road to the East by which Alexander's troops reached home from the Indus, passes through the Persian Gulf and along the river Euphrates. Should this important route be adopted, a canal already existing between the Tigris and Euphrates could be widened, another canal or railway line built between the Euphrates and the port of Iskanderoon, and the whole journey from England to the Punjab completed in 40 or 50 days.

ASIA.
TARTARS.
RUSSIAN PEASANTS.
THE WALRUS
PETRA.
SUN-BIRDS OF INDIA AND THE PHILIPPINE ISLES
ARCTIC OCEAN
NORTH PACIFIC OCEAN
INDIAN OCEAN
ARABIAN SEA
BAY OF BENGAL
CHINESE SEA
YELLOW SEA
SEA OF JAPAN
SEA OF OKHOTSK
KAMTCHATKA OR BHERINGS SEA
ALEUTIAN ISLES
MEDITERRANEAN SEA
BLACK SEA
CASPIAN SEA
PERSIAN GULF
RED SEA
EUROPE
AFRICA
AMERICA
RUSSIAN EMPIRE
SIBERIA
CHINESE EMPIRE
MONGOLIA
MANCHOURIA
INDEPENDENT TARTARY
TURKEY
ARABIA
PERSIA
CABOOL
AFGHANISTAN
BELOOCHISTAN
HINDOOSTAN
TIBET
BORNEO
PAPUA OR NEW GUINEA
SUMATRA
JAVA
CELEBES
PHILIPPINE ISLES
CAROLINE ISLES
Tropic of Cancer
Equator
Great Sandy Desert
SCALE
Longitude East 90 from Greenwich

Asia

Area and Physical Aspect

This vast continent is bounded on the north by the Arctic Ocean, on the east by the Pacific, on the south by the Indian Ocean and on the west by Europe and the Mediterranean. The maximum distance from east to west is about 7,000 miles, and from north to south 5,000 miles. The area has been variously estimated, but Hassel's calculation of 20,433,205 English square miles is probably nearest to the truth. The central regions of the continent form a vast elevated plateau of more than 3,000,000 square miles. This is supported by the Altai, Himalaya and Inchin Kingan mountains, from which several great rivers flow. The Altai have not been accurately measured but the highest peaks lie above the limits of perpetual snow. The Himalaya are the loftiest range on earth, with peaks from 20,000 to 26,852 feet. Asia contains every variety of climate from the frozen region to the equator; over large parts of the south there are abundant periodic rains and luxuriant vegetation.

Lakes and Rivers

Notwithstanding its size, there are no lakes in Asia of an extent and depth comparable to those of North America. The principal inland sea is the Caspian, whose waters have a bitter, salt taste attributed to the naphtha which impregnates the surrounding country. Its greatest ordinary depth is around 520 feet, although in one place soundings were not found with a line of 2,889 feet. There are several other lakes to be found in China, India, Persia and Tibet, and most are salt or bitter. Asia has many rivers of great length, the longest being the Yang-tse-kiang (3,000 miles) and the Obi (2,600 miles).

Volcanic Region

From Kamschatka in the far north-east to the Moluccas there is a continued volcanic line so active in the north that violent earthquakes continually alter the surface of the land and throw up new islands out of the sea.

Animal and Vegitable Kingdoms

The largest and most ferocious animals of the world are to be found in Asia: the elephant, rhinoceros and tiger in India, Birmah, etc.; the camel, buffalo and wild horse in Persia, Arabia, Tibet and the great central plateau. Wolves and jackals also abound. The vegetable kingdom is rich and varied, with tea, coffee, cotton, silk, tobacco, opium and rice all grown. The hardest and largest timber are also products of Asia.

Population

Asia was the cradle of the human race and is now the most populous division of the globe. Estimates of the total number vary from 500 to 580 millions. The peoples are roughly divided into four great races: the Caucasian, Mongolian, Malayan and Ethiopian. There are 937 Asiatic dialects, some based on a Sanscrit root, others on Arabic and Chinese. The main religions are Buddhism, Brahminism, Islamism, Christianity, Shamanism and Sikh. Great empires exist in China, Russia, Turkey, Persia, Birmah, Siam, Cochin China, Corea and Japan, and all except the last two have intercourse or diplomatic relations with the principal nations of Europe.

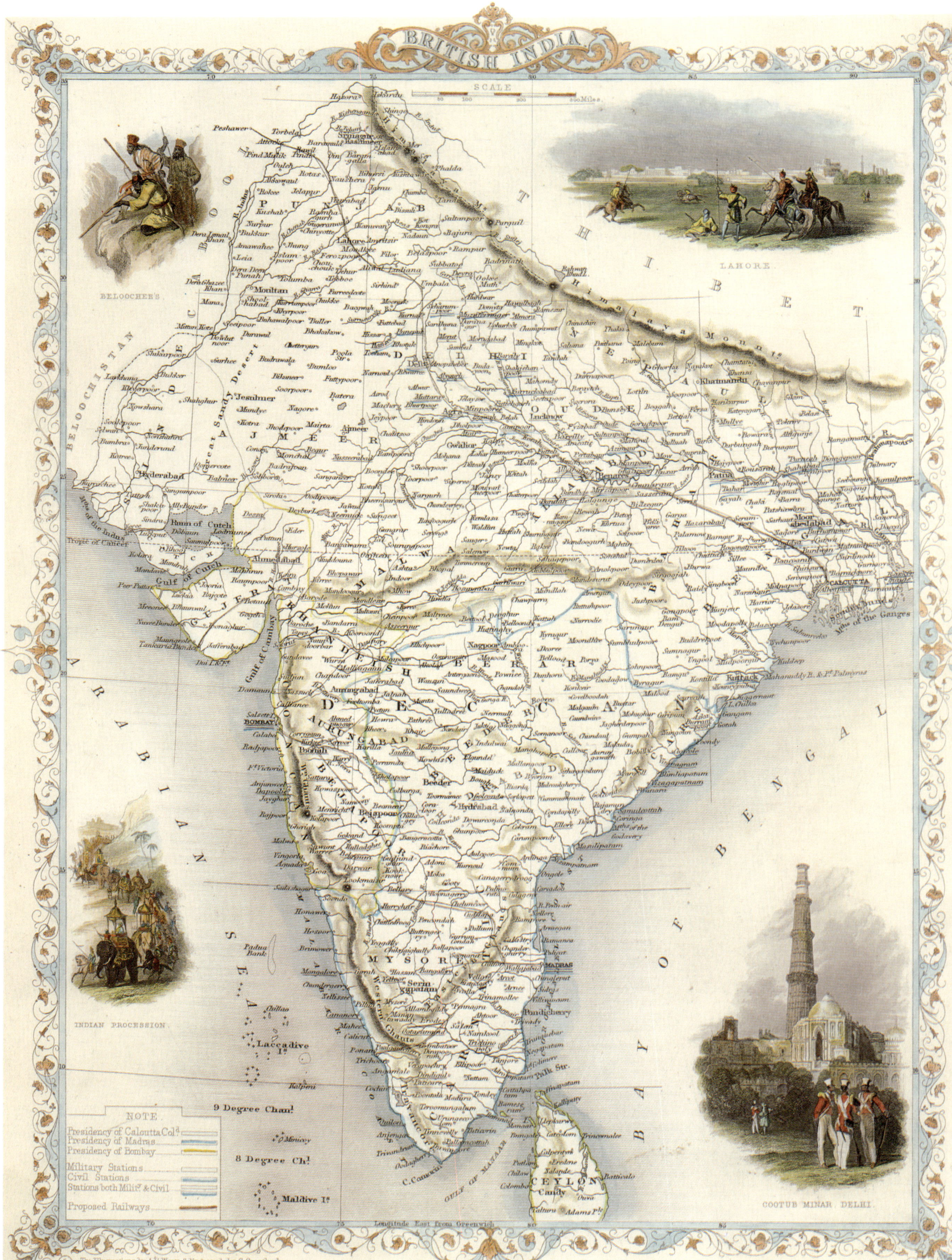

The Illustrations by A.H. Wray & Engraved by G. Greatbach.

The Map Drawn & Engraved by J. Rapkin.

British India

Area and Physical Aspect

No language would do justice to the varied and magnificent scenery of this great peninsula, which varies from inaccessible, snow-covered mountains to interminable plains intersected with deep and mighty rivers. It is estimated that 514 190 square miles are held in trust for the british crown by the East India Company (not including recently acquired countries in the Punjaub and Scinde), and a further 1,128,000 square miles of territories under the protection of the crown. The main mountain ranges are the Himalayas in the north, whose name means 'the abode of snow', and the less elevated Ghauts in the south-west. The most important rivers, many of them navigable for long distances, are the Indus (1,700 miles), the Ganges (1,500), the Jumna (780), these three all being extended by several tributaries. The climate is very various, according to latitude and elevation. At Simla, in the Himalayas, it is delightfully cool during the periods when the southern plains are scorched with a hot wind and a tropical sun.

History

The earliest authentic European account of Hindoostan is given of Alexander's armies pushing across the Punjaub. For a long period much of the country was under the all-pervading sway of the victorious Moslems headed by Tamerlane. The first Europeans to reach India by sea were the Portuguese, who secured themselves in Goa on the Malabar coast. The Dutch, French and English followed; and at the end of the sixteenth century Queen Elizabeth granted a charter to the East India Company, which has been responsible for acquiring a large part of British India.

Population

No regular census of the whole territory has been made, although it is vaguely estimated to contain about 100 million British subjects and a further 50 million allies. Of the British subjects, 70 million are supposed to be Hindoos of various castes, 20 million Mohamedans and 10 million Jains or Buddhists and other sects. A large number of well-educated Englishmen find honourable and lucrative employment in India, some in the military and a smaller number in the civil service.

Government

A Governor-General of all India, aided by a small Council nominated by the authorities in England, has total control of the British subjects; while at the courts of the allied princes there are European residents who influence or superintend the affairs of the courts to which they are accredited. Those areas under the control of the East India Company are ruled by 24 directors of the company.

Military Defence

India has one of the best organized and disciplined armies of the world, all native regiments being officered by Europeans. In time of peace the total number of regular troops stands at 185,000 to 200,000, in the usual proportions of artillery, cavalry and infantry. The annual cost of the Anglo-Indian army is about ten million pounds.

Trade and Industry

Commerce is small in proportion to the resources of the country and could most usefully be developed. The chief exports are cotton, silk, coffee, pepper, indigo and tobacco.

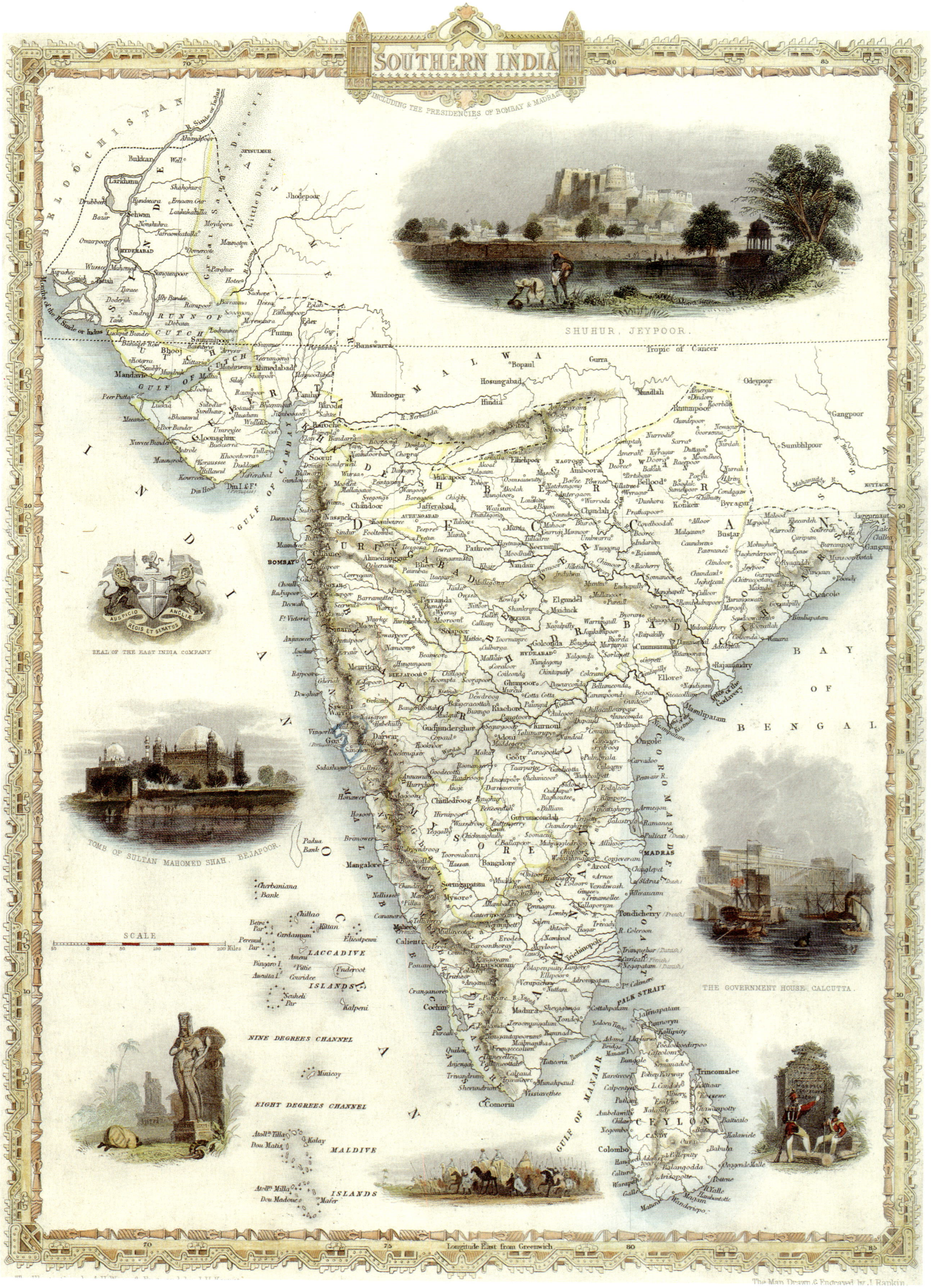

The Map Drawn & Engraved by J. Rapkin.

Southern India

The southern division of British India extends from the mouth of the Indus in the north-west eastwards to the Bay of Bengal and south to Cape Comorin and the Island of Ceylon. The accompanying map includes the presidencies of Bombay and Madras. Madras city, the capital of the presidency, is on the south-east coast and has no harbour. Bombay, the capital of the western presidency, has a fine haven and a strong fortress.

MADRAS PRESIDENCY governs an area unlike the alluvial plains and great river deltas of the north. It is divided into 18 territories. The Northern Circars extend along the west side of the Bay of Bengal. Throughout the lower Carnatic, the shore is flat and sandy, but from Cape Comorin up the Malabar coast the mountains in many places run close to the shore. Along this coast there are exquisite specimens of architecture to be found among the hills skirting the plain. The extensive table-land formed by the Ghauts is, for the greater part, under British dominion, and contains some of the most fruitful districts in the Madras presidency. The Mysore territory, an elevated plateau, is enclosed on two side by the East and West Ghauts, while Goorg, to the west of Mysore, is surrounded by lofty peaks, for the most part inaccessible, with highly cultivated valleys between. To the north of Bangalore the country falls rapidly. Hydrabad territory, embracing an area of nearly 10,000 square miles, consists principally of high granite ranges. The mountains are bare and rugged in outline. The soil and climate throughout the south are peculiarly suited to the production of sugar and every village has its patch of cane.

THE BOMBAY territories, including Poonah, Surat, Ahmedabad, Cutch, Candeish, and the territories in Scinde and in the Punjaub, constitute a large portion of the British dominions in India. The north-west quarter of the Deccan is divided by the natives into the Mawhuls, or hilly tracts, and the Desh, or flat country. Travelling south through the Deccan there are chains of flat-topped hills, although few exceed the moderate height of 1,500 feet. Their sides are covered with numerous blocks of trap rock which give them a tabular arrangement, as though they were fortified.

Many parts of the country are in the possession of Indian princes who first became connected with the Britain by subsidiary alliances. Some then ceded territories in return for military protection, while others lost their dominions by fortunes of war, and yet others were taken into British control because of the tyranny of their rule. Those princes who retain their independence now enjoy stipends paid to them from out of the public revenues (the Rajahs of Malabar, for example, receive a stipend of 2,500,000 rupees). They are allowed to exercise sovereignty over their tenants on their household lands, are exempted from the jurisdiction of the British courts of law, have their own civil and military functionaries, with all the insignia of state, and a British envoy, whose duties chiefly relate to their pecuniary affairs, or the ceremonials of sovereignty.

NORTHERN INDIA
INCLUDING THE PRESIDENCY OF CALCUTTA
SEAL OF THE EAST INDIA COMPANY.
CAR OF JUGGERNAUT
THE BRITISH RESIDENCY, HYDERABAD.
SCALE.
TIGER HUNT
RUINS, OLD DELHI.
HINDOOS
REFERENCE.
British Possessions.
States under British Protection.
Independent States.
Longitude East from Greenwich
LAHORE
THIBET
BHOTAN
SILHET
Lassa
Lake Palteh
Runn of Cutch
GULF OF CAMBAY
CALCUTTA
Mouths of the Ganges

Northern India

This division extends from the Himalaya mountains to Cuttack in the Bay of Bengal, and from the mouth of the Ganges to the Gulf of Cambay. It includes the presidency of Calcutta. Northern India can be divided into 5 districts: Bengal, Bahar, Orissa, the Ultra Gangetic province; and the North West provinces. Generally speaking the largest rivers and the most elevated regions are in the north of India. After the Himalayas one of the highest districts is Ajmeer or Rajasthan, where the surface is exceedingly varied. Many of the largest cities within the British territories are within Northern India, and in these towns and their environs education is being rapidly extended to native students.

BENGAL, containing 100,000 square miles, has scarcely a hill of any elevation. No country is better irrigated, the whole country being intersected by the Ganges, Brahmaputra, Hooghly, and many other rivers and tributaries which frequently change their beds and cause large stagnant marshes. The coastal area of Cuttack is similar to the contiguous delta of Bengal where the flat shore extends nearly 200 miles inland in a vast extent of country called the Sunderbunds, an interminable labyrinth of salt-water lakes, interspersed with mangrove islets. The chief city is Calcutta, the seat of the Supreme Government of British India, which stands on the banks of the Hooghly river In 1717 Calcutta was a straggling village, but it has now grown into a city of palaces with about 1,000,000 inhabitants.

BAHAR, containing 54,714 square miles, is a beautiful hill and dale country, apart from the flat north of the region. The soil is fertile, but less well watered than Bengal.

THE NORTH WEST PROVINCES: Allahabad, an area of 21,000 square miles, is under the sway of the king of Oude, and despite being one of the most fertile parts of India, most of its population of 6,000,000 are immersed in poverty and wretchedness. Lucknow, the capital, is 650 miles from Calcutta and a city of extraordinary oriental magnificence. The district includes Benares, the Holy City, which stands on the banks of the sacred river Ganges. Agra province is flat and open to the north-east but hilly and jungly to the south and west. The city of Agra on the river Jumna is a large fortress, forming one of the keys of Western India, particularly since it controls the navigation of the Jumna. Delhi province embraces the north part of the slope forming the plains of Hindoostan. Delhi city, the ancient capital of the Patan and Mogul empires, once covered an area of 20 square miles.

THE ULTRA GANGETIC PROVINCES of Tavoy, Ye, and Tenasserim were ceded to the British after the Burmese war and form a strip of land on the eastern side of the Bay of Bengal embracing a total area of about 15,000 square miles. Full of creeks, rivers and islets, the country is less swampy than Bengal or Cuttack, but diversified with hill and dale and rising towards the Siamese mountains with ranges of hills clothed with teak forests shelving towards the sea.

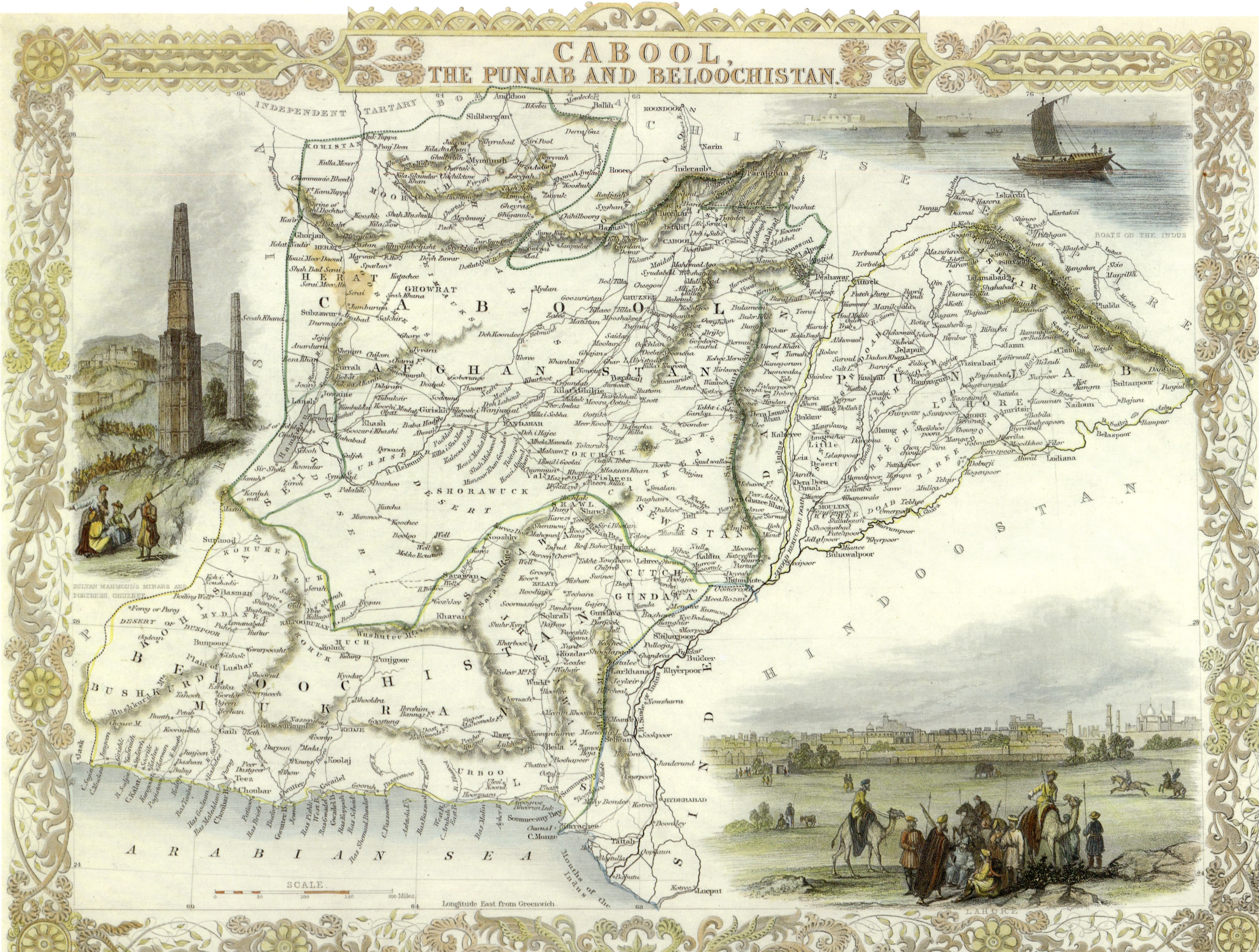

CABOOL,
THE PUNJAB AND BELOOCHISTAN.
INDEPENDENT TARTARY
BOATS ON THE INDUS
SULTAN MAHMOUD'S MINARS AND FORTRESS, GHUZNEE.
LAHORE.
CABOOL
AFGHANISTAN
BELOOCHISTAN
PUNJAB
HINDOOSTAN
CHINESE
ARABIAN SEA
HERAT
CANDAHAR
SHORAWUCK DESERT
SEWESTAN
CUTCH GUNDAVA
MUKRAN
SINDE
LAHORE
HYDERABAD
Months of the Indus
SCALE
Longitude East from Greenwich

Cabool, The Punjab and Beloochistan

THE PUNJAB, so called from two Persian words meaning five rivers, is an area of 125,000 square miles. The northern parts of the territory are mountainous with peaks up to 27,000 feet high, the lower plains are washed by the rivers Sutlej, Ravee, Chenab, Jhelum and Indus, which provide an inland navigation of nearly 2,000 miles. The climate is cold and bleak in winter and excessively hot in summer. At Lahore, in a tent well cooled, the thermometer stands at 112° in June. Vegetation is neither extensive nor varied. The more important crops are maize, millet and rice. Milk, butter and wool are great objects of rural economy, and there is considerable manufacturing activity.

The population, including that of Kashmere and Ladakk, numbers about 4,740,000; of these about 500,000 are true Singh (Lion) Sikhs, the remainder being ordinary Sikhs, Mahomedans, Hindoo and other denominations. The Sikh sect was founded by a Hindoo named Nanac in 1469. Originally peaceful, they finally drew the sword on the murder of their fourth guru in succession to Nanac and have never sheathed it. Guru Govind (tenth in succession from Nanac) founded their temporal power, directed his followers always to carry arms, and to assume the name Singh, only previously borne by the Rajpoots. In recent times the Sikh army has been trained and equipped by some of the ablest French and Italian officers of Napoleon's army, making it a formidable fighting force of at least 27,000 infantry and 27,000 cavalry.

The Singh Sikhs are mostly congregated about Lahore, the capital of the Punjab, whose population of about 100,000 is less than one-tenth of what the city and suburbs contained in the time of the Mogul emperors. Amritsir is larger, wealthier and more populous than Lahore and it was here that Runjeet Singh, the last great Sikh leader, kept his mint and treasure, estimated before his death at £30,000,000. Both cities are protected by large forts. Moultan city is of great antiquity, and is probably the Malli of Alexander. Originally one of the largest provinces of the Mogul empire, which included Bellochistan, Scinde, Swhestan, Tatta and Bhakr, the Moultan territory is now considerably reduced. Since its capture by the Sikhs, the city has lost much of its former wealth and prosperity, although it is still famous for manufactures of brocaded silks and rich carpets.

AFFGHANISTAN extends 660 miles from east to west, and 500 from north to south. Four-fifths of the country consists of rocks and mountains interspersed with desolate, barren table-lands and valleys of great fertility. The principal river is the Cabool, but generally the country is deficient in water. The celebrated Kyber pass, which is the north gate of India, is about 50 miles long with parts of the road cut out of the solid rock, and parts very steep and rough. The capital, Cabool is situated on the river of that name and has fertile and beautiful country around. Kandahar, a walled city southwest of Cabool commands the southern route from India to Persia.

PERSIA
KURDS
PERSIAN
BACTRIAN CAMEL
SCALE
CASPIAN SEA
INDEPENDENT TARTARY
RUSSIA
TURKEY IN ASIA
ARABIA
PERSIAN GULF
SEA OF OMAN
OMAN
KHORASAN
GREAT SALT DESERT
MAZANDERAN
KERMAN
LARISTAN
BELOOCHISTAN
ARDELAN
KIRMANSHAH
TEHRAN
ISPAHAN
Longitude East from Greenwich

Persia

Area and Physical Aspect

This ancient kingdom, known at different times as Iran, Elam, Media and Parthia, comprises about 450,000 English square miles. At its greatest length, from Mount Ararat in the north-west to the Sea of Oman in the south-east, the distance is about 1,300 English miles. The centre of the country constitutes an elevated plain, 2,500 to 4,500 feet above the sea, from which several mountain ranges rise. One ridge, the Tealish range, runs from east to west on the south of the Caspian Sea, and another, a branch of the Taurian range, runs roughly north to south. The interior is bleak, bare and arid, with villages and trees seen only on the banks of streams; but the provinces bordering the Caspian Sea are as beautiful as water, wood and mountain can make them. Four great deserts form part of the great Cobi, or naked desert, which stretches across Asia, with intermissions, from China to Arabia. Probably not a third of the area of Persia is cultivable. There are more than 30 salt lakes with no outlets. The capital is Tehran. Tabreez, the chief city of Azerbijan (population 100,000), is said to be the ancient capital of the Medes. Its citadel is now a large arsenal and a foundry has been established there for casting cannon. It is a centre for traders from many countries.

History

Originally inhabited by several independent tribes, Persia was a powerful monarchy in the days of Abraham, 1921 BC. For centuries the Persians were at war with the Assyrians, their neighbours, but they were finally conquered by Alexander the Great. A rebellious tribe, the Parthians, broke away from the Greeks and founded their own kingdom, which grew and prospered, particularly under Artaxares. Defeated by the Moslems, Persia then fell prey to successive conquerors, until the present dynasty was established by Nadir Kooli (died 1747). Britain enlisted the aid of the Persians in attacking the Affghans in 1799, and since that period the sovereigns of Great Britain and of Persia have been in friendly alliance, with large sums of money paid as subsidies to the Persian government.

Population

There are numerous estimates, all vague, and the true figure is probably between eight and ten million, of whom about 2,000,000 are nomadic. Religion is Mahomedan, of the sect of Alee or Sheeahs. The system of government is despotic; a royal edict can never be repealed and the word of the Shah, or king, is irrevocable. Modern Persia is divided into seven regions corresponding to the ancient areas of the Medes, Parthians, Hyrcanians, etc.

Trade and Industry

Persia has little commerce with western Europe. Formerly there was considerable trade between British India and the Persian Gulf coast, and also from England to Persia via Trebisonde in the Black Sea, but both these branches of commerce have declined and the principal trade is now with Russia. Horses are the best product and wherever water can be obtained for irrigation flowers and fruit abound.

ARABIA.

The Illustrations by H. Warren, & Engraved by J. Rogers.

The Map Drawn & Engraved by J. Rapkin.

Arabia

Area and Physical Aspect

This ancient and celebrated country forms an irregular quadrangle of about 1,100,000 square miles at the south-west extremity of Asia. It can be divided into Arabia Petrea in the north, Arabia Deserta in the east, and Arabia Felix in the west. A great plateau, supported on all sides by immense mountain buttresses, Arabia contains vast tracts of sandy desert.

History

Before the birth of Mahomet, different parts of Arabia were variously possessed by petty chieftains, the Abyssinians and the Persians, The rapid Progress of Islamism after the century extended the dominion of Mahomet's followers, the Khaliffs, from India to Spain, and the seat of power was moved from Arabia to Damascus. Although the authority of the Egyptian sovereign is now partially acknowledged along the borders of the Red Sea, most of the country is under the control of independent chiefs or sheiks.

Chief Districts

Arabia Petrea, now an arid region, was once the seat of splendid Roman towns. The cavernous and rock-bound city of Petra, formerly the capital of Idumea, was hewn entirely out of the sides of a mountain of solid porphyry, and its ruins are still in a fine state of preservation. The highest peak in the region is Mount Sinai (7,530 feet), at whose feet stands the Greek convent of St Catherine, and on whose summit there are a mosque and a dilapidated Christian church. The Hedjaz, or holy land of the Moslems, lies along the coast of the Red Sea. Mecca, the birthplace of the prophet, and Medina, the site of his tomb, are great centres of pilgrimage in this region. To the west of Mecca is Jiddah, the most active commercial port on the Red Sea and a fortified town. The finest province in Arabia is Yemen, an area of about 53,000 square miles, with 2,5000,000 inhabitants. One of its chief towns, Aden, is now occupied by the British. Nedjid, the largest province, has some excellent pastures where the finest horses in the world are reared, although much of its area is untenanted and waterless desert. Oman province is little known, but its capital, Muskat, has an excellent harbour, and the Imaum of Muskat has dominions extending down the coast of eastern Africa. Bahrain is noted chiefly for pearl and coral fisheries. Along 350 miles of the Persian Gulf lies an area known as the pirate coast, studded with islands, coves, bays and rocky shallows. In 1819 the British government destroyed the strongholds of the pirates and made a treaty with their chief. They differ much from the Bedouins, and appear to have some African blood in their veins.

Population

The people are a multitude of tribes, which can be divided into the Arabs of the Desert, or Bedouin, and the Arabs of the Cities. These two groups seldom intermarry. There is no possibility of ascertaining the total number of inhabitants, which has been variously estimated at between 10 and 12 million. Their hospitality is proverbial.

TURKEY IN ASIA
BLACK SEA
CASPIAN SEA
MEDITERRANEAN SEA
PERSIAN GULF
ASIA MINOR
ARMENIA
KOORDISTAN
ALGEZIRA
IRAK ARABI
SYRIA
ARABIA
ARABIA PETRÆA
EGYPT
ISTHMUS OF SUEZ
MOUTHS OF THE NILE
RUSSIA
PERSIA
TURKEY IN EUROPE
SYRIAN DESERT
CYPRUS
CONSTANTINOPLE
SMYRNA
ALEPPO
DAMASCUS
BAGDAD
BASRA
JERUSALEM
THE CASTLES OF EUROPE AND ASIA
SCALE
Longitude 38 East from Greenwich

Turkey in Asia

The territory in Asia over which the sultan of Constantinople holds sway extends from the Bosphorus to the Persian Gulf, a distance of 1,500 miles, and from Suez to Trebisonde, 1000 miles. In many places, however, the sultan's sovereignty is now soweakened as to be little more than nominal. Asia Minor, Syria and Palestine are described in separate maps. We shall therefore confine ourselves here to Armenia, Algezira, Koordistan and Irak-Arabi.

ARMENIA is distinguished by five distinct parallel mountain ranges. On its south-eastern border is the celebrated Mount Ararat, venerated by the natives, as well as by Christians and Jews everywhere as the mountain of Noah. The peak, probably some 20,000 feet high, rises from a base of 400 square miles area. Volcanic in origin, in 1840 Mount Ararat was shaken by some kind of eruption which poured torrents of melted snow from the slopes, devastating the country to a distance of seven miles. The Armenians were converted to Christianity by Gregory, but do not appear to have had an alphabet until the fifth century. They subsequently embraced the Eutychian heresy and are now independent from both Greece and Rome. Erzeroum, the capital has an extensive trade with Persia, Russia and the other cities of Asiatic Turkey. Armenia's total population is estimated at 2,000,000.

ALGEZIRA, or Mesopotamia, is divided from Armenia by a range of high mountains. Its name means 'region between the rivers' and the Euphrates forms its western border, while the Tigris flows 350 miles along the east of the country. Once a rich, fertile and luxuriant region, it is now sterile and sandy, except in the immediate vicinity of rivers. Urfah is supposed to be the site of Ur, home of Abraham, whose name is revered by Mahomedans, Christians and Jews alike. Together with Mousul and Diarkebir, the capital of a small pachalic of the same name, Urfah has a considerable trade with Aleppo, carried on by means of caravans, some with as many as 5,000 camels, each carrying at least 500 lbs.

KOORDISTAN between Mesopotamia and Persia is a mountainous and rugged country, and home to the Koords, estimated at just over one million. The Turkish Koords are a settled race, while the Persians Koords are nomadic and predatory. The people live in a feudal state, each village having a chief whose authority is acknowledged only so long as he is able to enforce it. Mahomedanism is here blended with the Magian and Manichean systems, and there are about 100,000 Nestorian Christians.

IRAK-ARABI is an extensive but deserted region, inhabited by hordes of wandering Arabs. The Turkish pachalic of Bagdad includes the regions anciently known as Babylonia, Chaldea, and a great portion of Assyria. Bagdad city has a population of about 65,000 and is well situated on the banks of the Tigris, about 190 miles above its junction with the Euphrates. Basra, near the head of the Persian Gulf, is a city of great commercial importance and five days sailing by steam vessel from Bombay.

ASIA MINOR
BLACK SEA
MEDITERRANEAN SEA
TURKEY IN EUROPE
SEA OF MARMARA
OLYMPUS.
RHODES.
SCALE.
Longitude East from Greenwich
TREBISONDE
KASTAMUNI
ANGORA
SIVAS
RUM OR SIVAS
KARAMANIA
ADANA
ALEPPO
DIYARBEKR
DIAR MODZAR
MARASH
MALATIA
MENTESHA
CYPRUS
SMYRNA
CONSTANTINOPLE
GULF OF ADALIA
GULF OF ISKENDEROON
ANTAKIA BAY

Asia Minor

Area and Physical Aspects

The peninsula termed Asia Minor to distinguish it from Asia Major, or Continental Asia, possesses great interest from its ancient historic associations, its commanding position, noble havens, beautiful scenery, rich soil and salubrious climate. Estimated at an area of 151,699 square miles, excluding Cyprus and the smaller islands, the country consists mainly of a wide-spreading table-land sloping westward of the Euphrates, which is almost surrounded by chains of mountains. The shores of the Mediterranean and Black Seas are bordered by a succession of narrower plains. The northern division is very beautiful, the southern less attractive and bounded by the steep and rugged Taurus range, whose highest peaks are at least 10,000 feet. The peninsula is very subject to earthquakes. During the reign of Tiberias Caesar, thirteen cities were destroyed in one day. Mount Olympus, near Brussa, emits a constant bright flame of ignited hydrogen gas. There are numerous lakes, many of them more or less impregnated with salt.

History

In ancient times Asia Minor was divided into several independent states, of which Phrygia was the chief. It was subsequently occupied by the Lydians, Persians, Macedonians, Syrians and Romans. Since the eleventhcentury it has been in the possession of the Turks. Three of the 'wonders of the world' were to be found in Asia Minor, but now even the sites of many of its once great cities are unknown. The present population of 7,584,950 is probably much reduced from ancient times. About three-fourths of the inhabitants are Mahomedans.

Harbours and Islands

The western and south-western shores abound in secure havens sheltered by numerous islands. The chief of these latter are Cyprus, Rhodes, Scarpanto, Lesbos, Scio and others in the Hellespont and Aegean Sea. The important ports are at Trebisonde on the Black Sea, which has of late years become the chief depot of trade between Asia and eastern Europe; Scutari in the sea of Marmara; and Smyrna on the west coast, the principal port of maritime traffic in all Asia Minor.

Climate and Productions

Except where marsh malaria prevails, Asia Minor is generally very salubrious and capable of yielding the chief productions of both the temperate and the torrid zones. Opium is largely produced and extensively consumed by the Turks. Angora in Galatia is famed for its fine breed of goats and cats, whose size and fineness of hair are well known. Iron and copper are plentiful, and gold and silver are found in several places.

Chief Places

Of the numerous wealthy and commercial cities which once studded the shores, bays and gulfs of the ancient kingdoms of Caria, Doria, Aeolia and Ionia, scarcely even a vestige remains. Apart from the ports, the chief towns are now Konieh (anciently Iconium), Angora, in the very centre, and Kara Hissar. In many places the ruins of large Christian churches are to be seen mingled with Pagan temples and tombs; and each district has a peculiarity in the architecture of its tombs, some being carved directly out of the rock.

SYRIA.
BAGGAGE CAMELS
ARABS
JERUSALEM
SCALE
Longitude East from Greenwich
MEDITERRANEAN SEA
CYPRUS
Nicosia
Famagosta
Larnica
C. St Andreas
DIYARBEKR
Diyar-bekr
Mardin
Urfah
Harran
Fez Oglu
Adiyaman
Somisat
Birehjik
Aintab
Marash
Kilis
Tarsus
Karaman
Eregli
Mout
Selefkeh
Iskenderoon
Antakia
ALEPPO
Rakkah
Hamah
Hums
TRIPOLI
Beirout
Saida
DAMASCUS
Tadmor (Palmyra)
SYRIAN DESERT
ARABIA
ARABIA PETRÆA
Jaffa
JERUSALEM
Gaza
Hebron
Jerash
Busrah
Mt. Carmel
el Arish

Syria

Area and Physical Aspect

The accompanying map of Syria includes the country anciently known as Phoenicia and Palestine, the whole being comprised within the dominions of Turkey. The entire area, estimated at 51,778 square miles, exclusive of the desert, is divided into four pachalics by the Turks: Aleppo, Tripoli, Acre, and Gaza and Damascus. It is a varied region of mountains, valleys and plains the climate being cool and salubrious in the hills, dry and scorching in the plains and humid and unhealthy near the coasts.

Mountains

From the Gulf of Iskenderoon to Beirout an almost unbroken chain of mountains winds along the shores of the Mediterranean - at an average distance of 25 miles from the sea. Near Antioch rises the extraordinary peak of Mount Cassiis, known by the natives as Bald Mountain because its summit is quite bare.

History

From the period when Richard the Lion-hearted contested the possession of the Holy Land with Saladin, Syria has remained under the domination of the Turks, and under their sway has declined in population, commerce and wealth. Before the discovery of the sea route to India Syria was a channel of trade between Europe and Asia; but the removal of this traffic and the consequent impoverishment of the country led to the disorganization of the eastern Turkish Provinces, and in 1831 Syria was invaded by the Egyptians. A joint European force assisted in the expulsion of the Egyptians and the restoration of Syria to the Turks in 1840.

Chief Towns

Aleppo and Antioch are greatly decayed from their former splendour. Antioch, especially, which was once the capital of Syria and second only to Rome, is now a wretched place. Aleppo is still a city of some trade, but was much injured by an earthquake in 1822, by which Antioch also was nearly overwhelmed. Damascus will be described with the map of Palestine.

Population

Having been successively conquered by the Assyrians, Babylonians, Persians, Macedonians, Romans, Arabs, Turks and Crusaders, the existing people are a most motley assemblage whose number it is almost impossible to estimate correctly. The predominating language spoken is Arabic, although old Syriac is confined to a few districts near Damascus, and a patois derived from Syriac and Chaldee is much used among the peasantry. The main religious groups are Mahomedan and Christian. The Mahomedans of Syria, constituting probably three-fourths of the whole population, occupy chiefly the agricultural districts and fill the public offices in the principal cities. There is a large body of Armenians in Syria, particularly at Aleppo and in the northern towns.

Commerce and Industry

The agricultural produce of Syria is small. The northern forests provide good quality timber in abundance. Cotton is grown and exported to Italy, France and Germany. The cultivation of silk has recently been spreading around Beirout, the greater part being sent to Genoa for the manufacture of velvets. Of late years considerable attention has been paid to the method of expressing Syrian oil, which appears likely to become a staple article of export.

ANCIENT PALESTINE
TOMB OF ABSALOM.
SYRIAN SHEEP.
CHURCH OF THE HOLY SEPULCHRE.
NAZARETH.
ANCIENT CEDARS OF LEBANON.
GREAT SEA
GALILEE
SAMARIA
JUDAEA
IDUMAEA
AMALEKITES
MOABITES
REUBEN
ABILENE
TRACHONITIS
ITURAEA
SIDON
TYRE
Damascus
Bahr el Merj
Mt. Hermon or Sirion
Waters of Merom
Bethsaida
Accho or Ptolemais
CAESAREA
Nazareth
Joppa or Japho
JERUSALEM
Bethlehem
Jericho
HEBRON
Ascalon
Gaza or Azzah
Beersheba
Rabbath Ammon
Ramoth Gilead or Ramoth Mizpeh
Ar or Rabbah
Ashtaroth
Bostra
THE SALT SEA, Sea of the Plain, the East Sea, Lacus Asphaltites (Dead Sea)
Wilderness of Edom
Desert of Zin
Longitude East from Greenwich
SCALE
Miles

Ancient Palestine

Boundaries

In the 34th chapter of Numbers, the limits of the Land of Canaan are specifically declared, but the difficulties of translating the Hebrew language in a matter involving minute topographical detail render the text very obscure and prevent us forming any accurate estimate of this country. Mount Hor in the Libanus chain evidently formed a feature of the northern border; Beersheba, the Wilderness of Edom and the Desert of Zin formed the southern frontier; the Dead Sea, the land of the Moabites, the Sea of Galilee and the Jordan constituted the eastern boundary. The western boundary was to be the Mediterranean, but the Jews did not succeed in expelling the Phoenicians and Philistines from the coastal area. For a very short period, the victories of David and Solomon appear to have extended the kingdom of Israel from the Mediterranean to the Red Sea and from the Euphrates to the frontiers of Egypt, but this enlarged dominion did not last long. The divisions, cities and towns marked on the map follow those indicated in the book of Joshua, in so far as they are known.

Rivers and Seas

The Jordan is the only river in Palestine which flows continually without drying up. Apparently formed by the union of two springs, it passes through the Sea of Galilee with a perceptible current and on to the Dead Sea, where it is absorbed. The Israelites are supposed to have crossed the Jordan near Bethabara at the head of the Dead Sea. The site now occupied by the Dead Sea, also called the Sea of the Plain, was formerly, in part if not wholly, a fertile and populous plain on which stood the cities of Sodom, Gomorrha, Admah and Zeboim.

Chief Cities and Towns

Jerusalem, the capital of Judea, is said to be the Salmem of which Melchizedec was king at the time of Abraham. It was built at distinct successive periods on a series of elevations of different heights. On the revolt of the ten tribes it ceased to be the metropolis of Israel, but was still the royal city of Judah and Benjamin. Jerusalem has been destroyed and rebuilt several times by successive invaders. The Romans eventually forbade the Jews right of entry, though this was restored to them by Constantine. Since the failure of the Crusaders to keep it, the city has been in Turkish hands. Jericho was situated in a plain of the same name. Now ruined, its original site has not been accurately identified. Samaria, the ancient capital of the revolted tribes was founded by Omri about the year 930 BC, destroyed by the Assyrians, and rebuilt by Herod the Great in 21 BC. Constantine's mother Helena built a great church there, whose ruins can still be seen. The famous cities of Tyre and Sidon were renowned as centres of maritime trade. Damascus, probably the oldest city in the world is said to have been founded by Uz, the grandson of Noah. Having been taken over by Israelites, Persians and Greeks, it eventually became the centre of the Mussulman world.

The Illustrations by H. Warren, & Engraved by R. Baker.

The Map Drawn & Engraved by J. Rapkin.

Modern Palestine

BOUNDARIES

Modern Palestine is under the dominion of the pachas of Acre and Damascus, the former ruling the coast, the latter the interior and by far the greater portion, including Jerusalem (El Khuds), El Khulil (Hebron), Nabulus (Shechem) and Tubariyeh (Tiberias).

MOUNTAINS

The mountains of Lebanon, the root of the whole mountain system of Palestine, are themselves ramifications of the great South Taurus range. Near the peak of Jebel Makmel is the sheltered recess containing the celebrated cedars whose extraordinary size has so long been the theme of travellers, No traveller has estimated the height of the loftiest summits in Lebanon, although they are probably more than 9,000 feet.

HOLY PLACES

The Mahomedans have of late greatly relaxed their hostility to the Jews and Christians; and since the expulsion of the Egyptians and the restoration of the Holy Land to the dominion of the Turks, the sultan of Constantinople has permitted the construction of a Christian church on Mount Sion and the creation of a bishopric in Jerusalem. At the spot on the Jordan river pointed out as the scene of our Lord's baptism, thousands of pilgrims are annually baptized. Bethlehem is a pleasant village, in the undisturbed possession of about 3,000 Christians. A rich altar is erected over the place where our Redeemer is supposed to have been born, and on Christmas morning a body of the villagers are wont to repair to the field consecrated by tradition as the place where the shepherds were keeping watch at the time of the Nativity. The Mount of Olives, in a general sense, is a range of hills east of Jerusalem, that from which our Saviour ascended into heaven being the centre of the three chief summits.

CHIEF CITIES AND TOWNS

Acre, a place of great strength, has for ages been viewed as the maritime key of Palestine and undergone many sieges and assaults since the year 636, when it was taken from the Christians by the Saracens, to its recent capture by the English from the Egyptian troops under Ibrahim Pacha. Modern Damascus, also designated the 'City of Joy' and the 'eye of the east', is estimated to have a population of 200,000. In the centre of the city stand a spacious bazaar, eight synagogues, one Latin and three Franciscan convents, four churches, and about 200 mosques, the finest of which was once a church dedicated to St John of Damascus. Jerusalem is still a walled city and from its position is well calculated for the capital of Palestine. Its population fluctuates in number, but is presently estimated at about 20,000 of whom one quarter are said to be Christians.

POPULATION

Of the present number of half a million or so inhabitants, the Jews form but a small portion. The remainder consists of Mussulmen and members of the Roman Catholic, Greek and Syrian churches. The pure Jews are supposed to number between three and four million but broken and scattered over every land on the earth, they, as well as their country, remain a monument of the past.

The Illustrations by A.H. Wray, & Engraved by J.B. Allen.

The Map Drawn & Engraved by J. Rapkin.

China and Birmah

Area and Physical Aspect

The vast empire of China covers an area of five million square miles, of which only 1,500,000 constitute China Proper. There are three marked features: an elevated northern region on which Peking, the capital, is situated; an alluvial plain through which the Yang-tse-kiang and Yellow Rivers flow; and a broken, undulating country in the south with broad valleys and lofty mountains. The coastline from Chusan to the Yellow Sea is low and swampy, elsewhere it is bold and rugged. Two-thirds of China proper are studded with hills and ranges, and Chinese geographers enumerate 5,270 celebrated mountains, of which they say 467 yield copper and 3,609 iron. The north of the country is hot in summer and cold in winter. At Canton, snow is unknown. The heat in the southern districts is intense.

Rivers

The Yang-tse-kiang or 'Girdle of China' is said to be 2,283 miles long, and it is navigable for 200 miles from its mouth for the largest class vessels. By means of canals and lakes, this river is connected with the whole empire. The Hoang Ho, or Yellow River, is less navigable due to its low loose banks and rapid floods. These two great rivers are linked by the Transit River, a canal constructed in the fourteenth century.

The Great Wall

This enormous fortification was built in the third century BC to protect the Chinese from the incursions of the Tartars. It is 1,500 miles long, 20 to 25 feet high with 40-feet towers at intervals and has four great gates.

Population

The whole population of the empire is above four hundred millions, of whom 367,632,907 live in China Proper. Accurate figures are obtained from a census taken in one night on which every householder must fix to his door a board describing the name, sex and age of everybody in his house.

History

Chinese tradition dates back as far as 2204 BC, about 140 years after the flood. Their first great emperor must, according to their accounts, have been contemporary with Noah. Over the centuries, successive dynasties have reigned over the country, the present ruling family being Tartar in origin. Paper, printing, gunpowder, cannon, porcelain, the smelting and combination of metals, were all known in China many centuries before their introduction into Europe. In 166 AD Marcus Antoninus sent an embassy to China and between that time and the usurpation of the present dynasty in 1644 the country communicated freely with the rest of the world. The emperor rules despotically with a council of ministers whom he can choose not to consult. Recent hostilities between England and China about the opium trade have reduced British access to the Chinese ports.

Commerce and Industry

Canton is the chief seat of foreign commerce, and much trade is conducted with America and England, in addition to those many lands of the East in which the Chinese are located. The chief products are tea, silk, rice and quicksilver. The export of tea from China to England has now reached 50 million pounds.

The Illustrations by H. Winkles, & Engraved by G. Greatbach.

The Map, Drawn & Engraved by J. Rapkin.

Thibet, Mongolia, and Mandchouria

These extensive regions are colonies or dependencies of the Chinese empire and their area, boundaries, population, topography and products are very little known. Mr Wells Williams, an American missionary in China, has estimated their united area at 3,951,130 square miles.

THIBET is a region of mountain ranges and high plains, up to 10,000 feet above the sea. The number of peaks in this district above the line of perpetual snow is greater than that of any other part of the world of the same extent. The Indus, Yang-tze-kiang, and the Brahmaputra, three of the largest rivers in the world, all have their sources in Thibet. There are many lakes, the largest, Tengki-ri-nor, being situated in the midst of stupendous mountains north-west of Lassa. Some of these isolated waters are perfectly salt. Thibet's total area of about 530,000 square miles is divided into three provinces, Ladak being totally independent and Ulterior and Anterior Tibet being ruled by the Teshu-Lama and the Dalai-Lama, overseen by Chinese residents. The Dalai Lama, who resides in Lassa, the capital, is chief of the Buddhist religion. His residence is the convent of Pobrang-Marbu, a building 367 feet in height and with a myriad of rooms. The Chinese government maintains a strong garrison near the city, of which the population is about 25,000. The Thibetan climate is pure and so dry that mutton exposed to the air at certain seasons becomes dry enough to powder and preserve as 'flesh bread'. The total population of about 220,000 are of Mongol origin and considerably advanced in manufacture and mechanical arts. Polyandria prevails.

MONGOLIA, with an area of some 1,400,000 square miles, is divided into four provinces, some ruled by a Mantchu resident, some by their own chieftains. Generally elevated, the whole country is almost encircled by mountain ranges, with the great Gobi desert of sand in its centre. An ancient road crosses part of the desert and has for centuries been the route of mercantile communication between China and the western parts of Central Asia. The climate is excessively cold, due to the great elevation and want of shelter from the winds. North of the Gobi every month of the year sees some snow and frost. Since the soil is poor, the Mongols (numbering about 2,000,000) are chiefly nomadic. The Kalkas, or principal tribe, have their headquarters at Kurun, the largest town, and are devoted Buddhists.

MANDCHOURIA has been very little visited by Europeans. The great part of its 700,000 square miles is covered by forests, filled with bears, tigers, wolves and other fur-bearing animals, and the Chinese and Russians have several fur collecting forts in the northern districts of the province. The principal feature of Mandchouria is the great Saghalien river which, with its many tributaries, drains the whole eastern slope of Central Asia and flows an entire distance of 2,200 miles before entering the sea at the Gulf of Saghalien. The capital, Moukden, was once the seat of government of the Mantchu monarchs and is surrounded by a wall 10 miles in circuit with an inner wall containing the emperor's palace.

INDEPENDENT TARTARY
TARTARS ON A JOURNEY.
THE BRIDE CHASE.
A MARRIAGE CUSTOM OF THE TARTARS.
THE TENT.
SCALE
Longitude East from Greenwich
CASPIAN SEA
ARAL SEA
LAKE BALKACH OR TENGHIZ
KIRGHIZ MIDDLE HORDE
KIRGHIZ KHASAKS
GREAT HORDE
KOKAND
BOKHARA
KHAREM
KHIVA OR
DESERT OF KIZIL KOUM
DESERT OF KARA-KOUM
DESERT OF KHIVA OR KHAREM
KARA KALPAKS
USBEKS
TURKOMANS
SAROKS
SALORES
TUKAS
KOONDOOZ
KAFFIRSTAN
CABOOL
Orenburg
Ouralsk
Verkho Ouralsk
Troitsk
Orsk
Astrakhan
Mouths of the Volga
Astrabad
Mushed
Merve
Balkh
Bokhara
Samarkand
Kokand
Tashkend
Turkestan
Khiva
Kara Bughaz Gulf
Krasnovodsk
Cumberland
C. Apsherod
Kizil Agatch G.
Reshid
Saree
Kooohan
Boojnoord
Kelat
Merochak
Meimoona
Budakshan
Khooloom
Kizil Koum Desert
Kangour Desert
Batkak Koum Desert
Boukhan Hills
Alatau Mts
Mingboulak Mts
The Illustrations by W. Bragg & Engraved by J. Rogers.
The Map. Drawn & Engraved by J. Rapkin.

Independent Tartary

Area and Physical Aspect

Estimated at 846,000 square miles, this area to the east of the Caspian Sea is divided into many small Mohamedan states, subject to despotic chiefs termed khan. A large portion of the western region consists of immense desert plains of sand or clay, interspersed with fertile tracts in the basins of the Oxus, or Amoo, and Syr, or Sihoun, rivers. The Kerghiz steppes are undulating grassy plains, devoid of trees, which appear sterile, uniform and silent. Between the Caspian and Aral seas the soil is sandy or rocky and covered with shells, suggesting that the two seas were once one. The climate is severe, with spring appearing suddenly on the steppes, summer following dry and burning, and the winter long, dry and constantly cold.

Mountains

The Hindoo Kush range, separating Tartary from Persia and Affghanistan, has the loftiest peaks in the world, the highest estimated at 30,000 feet. The Bolor, to the south-east, are known by the Chinese as the 'Azure' or 'Shining' mountains from the quartz of which they are chiefly composed. The Mussar and Alatan ranges run south-east and north-east from the border with China. Of the more northerly ranges very little is known.

Rivers

The two most important are the Amoo and the Syr. The Amoo flows for 1,100 miles from the Hindoo Kush to the Sea of Aral, taking in many tributaries. At Bokhara it is 100 yards wide, and when swollen by melting snow expands to four miles. The Syr, also flowing into the Sea of Aral, flows mostly through a bare, treeless waste, the thickets of reeds on its banks affording shelter and fuel for Kerghiz encampments. This river marked the northern boundary of Alexander the Great's empire.

Chief Towns

Bokhara (population 250,000), centre of the ancient kingdom of Bactria, is a large and wealthy trading city to which caravans of several thousand camels travel from Persia, Cabool and other places. It abounds in mosques, roofed bazaars, colleges and caravanseras for the travellers. Samarcand (population 60,000), once a heavily fortified and noble city, was captured by Alexander, besieged by Gengis Khan and occupied by Sheebanee Khan, founder of the Usbec dynasty. Efforts are now being made to restore it. Khiva, the granary of the wandering hordes, is heavily defended. The khan there can bring 40,000 horsemen into the field.

Population

Tartar is a generic appellation given for six centuries to the nomadic tribes of Northern and Middle Asia, and now accorded by the Russians to the Asiatic races. When conquered by the Mongols under Gengis Khan, the Tartars became incorporated with his army, and the various peoples now occupying Tartary have sprung from this mixture. The Kerghiz and Turcoman tribes are nomadic tent-dwellers, keeping sheep and horses. The Turcomans, in particular, are proud horsemen who can travel long distances with little food or drink. The Usbecs are partly settled and strict Soonees of the Mahomedan faith. Their relative numbers are not exactly known, but the population for the whole area of Independent Tartary probably numbers less than ten million.

RUSSIA IN ASIA
ARCTIC OCEAN
NORTH PACIFIC OCEAN
N. AMERICA
BHERING STRAIT
GULF OF ANADIR
KAMTCHATKAN SEA
SEA OF OKHOTSK
JAPAN SEA
KOURILE ISLES
GULF OF TARTARY
SAGHALIAN
NOVA ZEMLIA
SEA OF KARA
GULF OF OBI
GULF OF BOTHNIA
G. OF FINLAND
WHITE SEA
Arctic Circle
EUROPE
SAMOIEDES
OSTIAKS
TOBOLSK
TOMSK
IENISSEISK
IAKOUTSK
IRKOUTSK
OKHOTSK
TCHOUKTCHIS
KAMTCHATKA
SIBERIA
INDEPENDENT TARTARY
CHINESE TARTARY
LIAKHOV ISLANDS
NEW SIBERIA
SKORSKARSKOI PAGOST
TROITSK
KAMTCHATKAN DOGS
SCALE
Longitude East 110 from Greenwich

Russia in Asia

AREA AND PHYSICAL ASPECT

This vast portion of the Russian Empire, stretching from the Ouralian Mountains to the Pacific Ocean, is known as Siberia and Kamtchatka. The 'Almanack de Gotha' for 1845 describes this wild and cheerless region as having an area of 3,625,000 square miles, and a population of 2,652,800 (less than one mouth per square mile). Western Siberia is divided into Tobolsk, Tomsk and Omsk, Eastern Siberia into Okhotsk and Kamtchatka.

HISTORY

In 1242 the Tartars founded the Khanete of Sibir. Ivan II nominally added Siberia to the dominion of the czars in 1563 and in 1587 Tobolsk was founded. After extending their rule along the Frozen Ocean to eastward and southward over the next century, the Russians fought a war with China in 1680, since which time Siberia and Kamtchatka have remained under Russian rule.

RIVERS

The Obi rises near the frontiers of China and flows through a great part of Tartary and Siberia, where it is joined by the Irtish, and then into the Arctic Sea. The Lena has a tortuous course of 2,500 miles from China to the Arctic Sea, and is safely navigable to Yakutzk. The Yennesei also rises in China and flows through Siberia for 2,500 miles into the Arctic Sea. The Amour, a noble river, flows a course of 1,800 miles.

PROVINCES

Tobolsk is a region of severe climate, with vast sandy tracts in the north where only low stunted brambles grow, and some grain-producing areas in the south. The chief town, also named Tobolsk (population 20,000), has wooden houses and wood-paved streets. It is the residence of the governor-general of Western Siberia and the Archbishop of all Siberia. Sibir, the ancient capital of the Tartars about 10 miles away is now in ruins.

Irkutsk, or Iakoutsk, covers more than half of Siberia and is divided into four districts: Irkutsk, Jakutsk, Kamtchatka and Tchoukotsk. The capital, also called Irkutsk (population 15,000), is a fine town with more than a dozen churches, an exchange and a superb saloon.

Okhotsk, which comprises the most eastern part of Siberia is a hilly country covered with marshy woods, so severe in climate that the port of Okhotsk is only open between July and October. The country of the Tchouktchis, extending west from the Bhering Strait, is a land of hunters and fishers who live in great poverty.

Kamtchatka is a long peninsula, 80,000 square miles in area, most of which consists of a chain of volcanic mountains, some of them still active. The winter lasts for ten months, with the ground being permanently frozen to a depth of 20 inches. Dogs are employed to perform all the draught required from horses in Europe. The small population of 6,000 are settled mostly along the west coast and engaged in fur-trapping, whaling and fishing.

Kiachta, the frontier town between Russian and China, is only three versts from the Chinese village of Maimadshin. The town ranks as a free port and has an elegant new market-place which cost over 1 million rubles to construct.

JAPAN & COREA
YEDO.
SEA OF JAPAN
YELLOW SEA
PACIFIC OCEAN
STRAIT OF COREA
NIPHON
KIOUSIOU
SIKOKF
COREA
STATE BARGE.
COREANS.
SCALE
Longitude East from Greenwich
Quelpaert
Corean Archipelago
Chosan Har.
Tsusima
Nangasaki
Swounada Sea
Tanegasima
Str. of Van Dimen
Str. of Matsmai
Matsmai
Port Nambu
Oki Is.
Sado
Broughton Bay
Futsisio (place of exile for the Grandees of Japan)

Japan, or Nipan, and Corea

JAPAN, an empire in itself, consists of a series of islands with a total area of 270,211 square miles. The principal islands are Niphon, Kiusin (or Keosew) and Sikokf, which form the centre of the chain. Little is known of the country, though the islands are deeply indented with secure harbours. The principal island is traversed by a volcanic chain of mountains, some covered with perpetual snow. The country is extraordinarily well cultivated and abounds in fine tea, gold and silver.

The origin of the Japanese people is obscure. Physically there is some resemblance with the Chinese but the Japanese are more advanced in the arts, sciences and literature, and their greater social freedom allows women a position scarcely inferior to that held by the fair sex in Europe. After several centuries of peace between China and Japan, from 100 BC to 600 AD, there followed almost a thousand years of intermittent hostility. Since the sixteenth century, however, no open war has been waged, although trade has been strictly regulated.

European intercourse with Japan commenced in 1542 when a Portuguese ship was wrecked in the province of Bungo. The Japanese allowed the Portuguese not only to trade and reside in the country but also to preach the gospel. Great
quantities of precious metals were exported and many Japanese were converted. Eventually, however, rivalry between Portuguese and Spanish missionaries alarmed the government. A rebellion, in which some of the Christian converts had taken part, was successfully repressed, and the Portuguese were finally expelled in 1635-40.

The Dutch, too, first came to Japan because of a shipwreck in 1599. The Dutch ship's pilot was an Englishman named Adams, who so pleased the Emperor that he granted the Dutch trade concessions which they still enjoy. In 1640, however, the Dutch were confined to the port of Nangasaki.

Adams was also responsible for the development of English intercourse with Japan. At his request, the East India Company carried a letter and presents from King James to the Emperor. In return England was accorded a treaty offering almost unlimited rights of trade, which has never been revoked. A factory was set up, but on Adams' death it was attacked by the Dutch, and the English fled, never since to reoccupy their position.

The present population of the country has been variously estimated at between 25 and 50 million people. They are governed by a celestial emperor, or high priest (Mikado), and a temporal sovereign (Seogun). There are 8 provinces, 622 districts and excellent municipal institutions.

COREA, a remarkable peninsula some 500 miles long and 300 or so broad lying between China and Japan, is imperfectly known, but reported to be a beautiful fertile country, abounding in useful products and containing about 20,000,000 inhabitants. The government is despotic, although the king receives a nominal investiture from China. The people are celebrated for their learning and are said to be friendly to Europeans. Hanching, the capital, has a river communication with the sea.

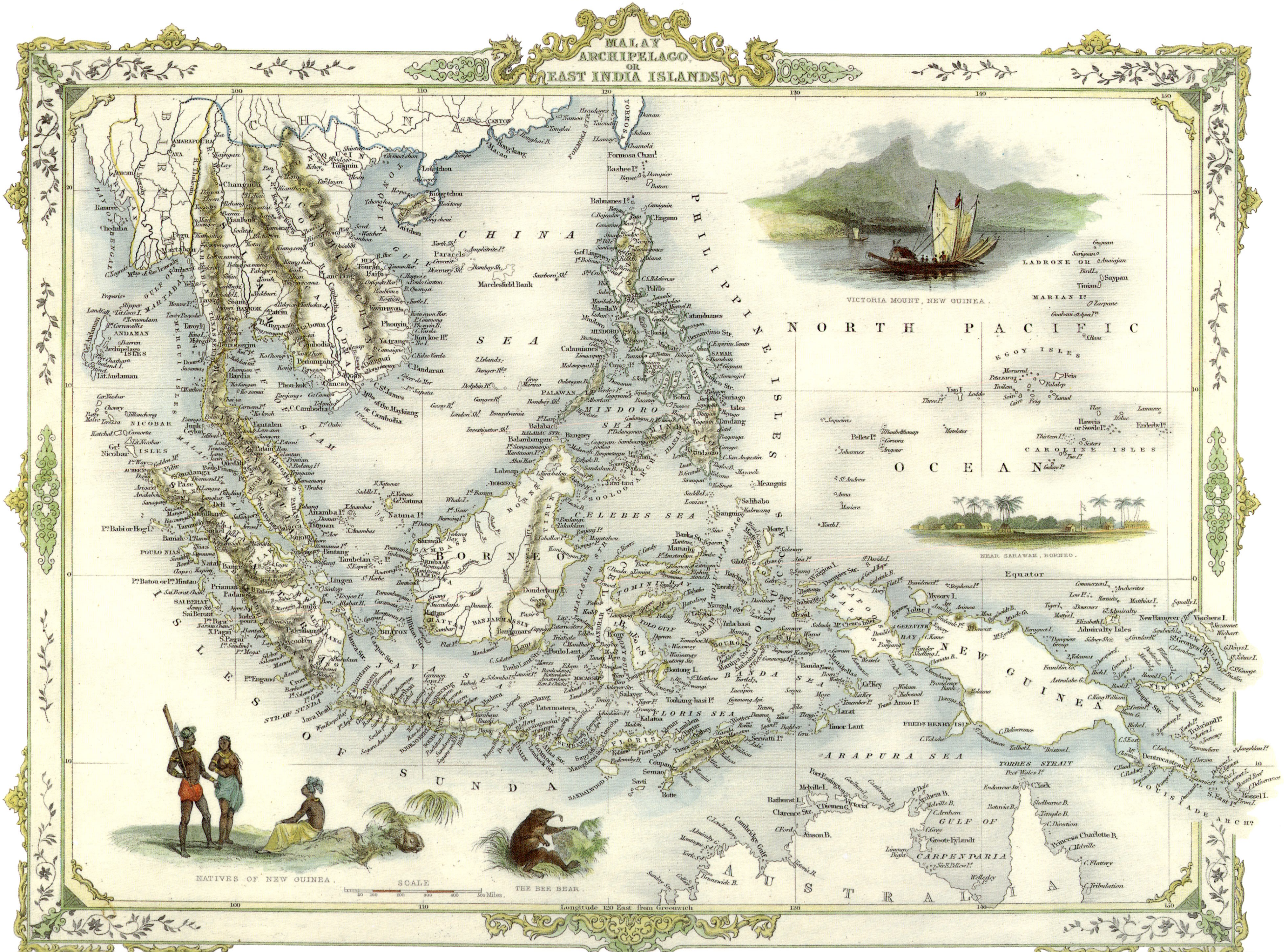

MALAY ARCHIPELAGO, OR EAST INDIA ISLANDS
CHINA SEA
NORTH PACIFIC OCEAN
PHILIPPINE ISLES
BORNEO
CELEBES
NEW GUINEA
AUSTRALIA
ISLES OF SUNDA
JAVA SEA
CELEBES SEA
MINDORO SEA
BANDA SEA
FLORIS SEA
ARAPURA SEA
GULF OF SIAM
GULF OF TONQUIN
GULF OF MARTABAN
BAY OF BENGAL
GULF OF CARPENTARIA
TORRES STRAIT
MACASSAR STR.
STR. OF SUNDA
LADRONE OR MARIAN IS.
CAROLINE ISLES
EGOY ISLES
LOUISIADE ARCH?
ANDAMAN ISLES
NICOBAR ISLES
MERGUI ISLES
FORMOSA
Equator
VICTORIA MOUNT, NEW GUINEA.
NEAR SARAWAK, BORNEO.
NATIVES OF NEW GUINEA.
THE BEE BEAR.
SCALE
Miles
Longitude 120 East from Greenwich

Malay Archipelago, or East India Islands

The accompanying map covers the continental regions between the Bay of Bengal and the North Pacific Ocean, and the Eastern Archipelago. However, lack of space precludes more than a brief allusion to the leading places.

BIRMAH is a hilly, well-watered, fertile and thickly peopled country about 560 miles long, by 300 broad. The Irawaddy river crosses it from north to south, reaching the sea at Rangoon, a trading port. The capital is Ava.

MARTABAN, TAVOY, TENASSERIM and the MEGU archipelago are governed for England. Mergui, the capital (population 10,000), is celebrated for teak and favourably situated for trade.

MALACCA peninsula is the land of the Malays, and extends for about 775 miles from north to south. Gold, iron and tin abound. There are three British settlements adjoining the Malacca Straits: Singapore is commercially remarkably successful, with a maritime traffic of about £10,000,000; Malacca Settlement has less trade but resources are numerous; Penang is a beautiful mountainous island, yielding largely spices and sugar.

SIAM, 250,000 square miles in area, is traversed from north to south by the river Meinam and bounded on east and west by a chain of mountains. It produces great quantities of sugar, rice, cotton, etc. Bankok, a large commercial city has some trade with Singapore.

LAOS is little known, but said to be elevated, healthy and abounding in metals. The Shan, or T'hay people frequent the great annual fair at Ava, bringing minerals, sugar, silk and lacquered ware.

CAMBODIA is traversed by the Cambodia river, said to be 1,500 miles long, on which Saigon, the capital, stands. Little is known of the country. COCHIN-CHINA has an area of 100,000 square miles. Hue, the chief sea-port, is well adapted for trade. Our commerce with this and the preceding three regions is very small.

PHILLIPPINE ISLANDS are under the dominion of the Spanish. About 40 in number, of which 13 are inhabited, these islands form a valuable group, productive in sugar, rice, silk and other commodities. Manilla, the capital, is on the largest island of Luzon.

BORNEO, an estimated 212,689 square miles in area, has central mountains sloping to alluvial and marshy tracts on the shore. The interior is populated by the Dyaks, with Chinese, Malays and others living on the coasts. Borneo abounds in plant and animal life and is rich in mineral products.

JAVA is traversed by a volcanic ridge of mountains up to 10,000 feet high, and is now a Dutch possession (population about 9,000,000). The scenery is beautiful beyond conception, the productions of sugar, coffee, tea and rice enormous.

SUMATRA, also Dutch, is divided into two equal parts by the equator. Some 130,000 square miles in area it is crossed by chain of volcanic mountains. Every kind of tropical plant grows here to enormous size. 45,000,000 lbs of pepper are annually exported. The population is scanty.

CELEBES is estimated to cover 55,000 square miles. It contains several active volcanoes. The Dutch have a fortress here. Rice and cotton, spices and timber abound, and there are rich gold mines.

ISLANDS IN THE INDIAN OCEAN

Islands in the Indian Ocean

MADAGASCAR, the largest island contiguous to Africa has an area estimated at between 150 and 200 million acres. The French navigator De Gonville is said to have discovered it in 1505-6. But it had long been known to the Moors, Arabs and eastern nations and is mentioned in the travels of Marco Polo as Magaster. A mountain chain with peaks rising to 12,000 feet passes from north to south throughout the island. The shore is low, swampy and unhealthy, but the inland elevated areas are covered with gigantic forests intersected by fast-flowing rivers. The population, formerly very numerous, now numbers about 5,000,000. There are many tribes or clans, but the people can be roughly divided into two races. There are no European settlements on the island. Cattle and sheep are numerous, cotton and flax of excellent quality are cultivated, and metals, including gold, abound.

MAURITIUS, 160 leagues to the east of Madagascar, has an area of 676 square miles. First discovered by a Portuguese navigator, it was temporarily settled and abandoned by the Dutch and then formally occupied by the French who made great improvements. Captured by the British in 1810 it has since remained part of the British empire. Exceedingly picturesque, the appearance of the island suggests that it was at one period an immense crater. The population of about 180,000 includes the old French inhabitants, the English, African blacks (formerly slaves) and Coolies from India. The staple product is sugar.

BOURBON, to the south-west of Mauritius is a French possession. The soil is very fertile and much sugar, coffee, etc is exported to France. The population is about 120,000, of whom half are negro slaves.

THE SEYCHELLES, to the northeast of Madagascar number fifteen islands, the largest of which is Mahe. Previously occupied by the French from Mauritius, they were ceded to Britain in 1810. They rest upon a coral bank, but are lofty, composed of granite and covered with verdure. There are many excellent harbours and the sea is ever tranquil. The chief products are sugar, coffee and spices.

THE LACCADIVE ISLANDS off the Coromandel coast belong partly to Britain and partly to her highness the Beebee Canamore. The main nine islands contain about 15,000 people, and occasionally suffer severely from hurricanes.

THE MALDIVE ISLANDS, more numerous than the Laccadives, are generally low and covered in vegetation, with many groves of coconut trees. The inhabitants are hospitable to ship-wrecked mariners.

SOCOTRA, to the east of Cape Guardafui, is little known but, appears to be as arid and barren, with stony soil and little water. The few inhabitants are chiefly Arab, the government patriarchal.

THE NICOBAR ISLANDS in the Bay of Bengal are generally low, covered in rank vegetation and unhealthy. Until recently the Danes had a settlement at Carnicobar, but it has now been abandoned.

THE ANDAMAN ISLANDS, to the north of the Nicobars, consist of the Greater and Lesser Andaman, the two islands being 40 miles apart. Both are lofty, clothed with timber and have good harbours.

CEYLON.
SCALE
50 Miles
LAKE OF KANDY.
ADAM'S PEAK FROM THE LAKE OF COLOMBO
RUINS OF A DAGOBA AT TOOPHARAMAYA.
TEMPLE OF BUDDHA KALANY
COLOMBO
Longitude East from Greenwich.
NORTHERN PROVINCE
WESTERN PROVINCE
EASTERN PROVINCE
SOUTHERN PROVINCE
CENTRAL PROVINCE
TAMBANKADEWA
VEDDAH
WELLASSEE
Adams Bridge
Rameseram
Jafnapatam
Trincomalee
Batticaloe
Anurajapoora
Kornegalle
Badulla
Alipoota
Ratnapoora
Hambantotte
Tangalle
Galle
Dondra Head
Caltura
Colombo
Negombo
Chilaw
Calpentyn
Putlam
Manaar
Point Pedro
Mooletivoe
Bintenne
Nallande
Kattragam

Ceylon

Area and Physical Aspect

Variously known as Singhala, Lanka, Serendib or Taprobane, Ceylon has a superficial area of about 24,664 square miles. The interior of the island is formed of ranges of high mountains from 1,000 to 4,000 feet, with an area of elevated table—land to the north and south of them. Between the mountains are some of the loveliest valleys the sun ever shone on, with placid rivers, magnificent cascades and all the beautiful verdure of the tropics.

History

The original Singhalese are probably descended from a colony of Singhs, or Rajpoots, to whom they bear a striking resemblance in appearance, 500 years BC. The Malabars several times invaded the island 200 years BC. Various remains of great antiquity, including canals, bridges, pagodas, many of them constructed without mortar from dovetailed stone, suggest the existence of great past civilizations. The gigantic pagoda of Batticaloa has a cone a quarter of a mile in circumference. In the sixth century Ceylon was the chief mart for eastern commerce, its central situation having led to its ports being frequented by ships from China, India and Arabia. When the Portuguese first visited the island in 1505, they found that it had been declining for a long period, due to wars and invasions' and soon acquired possession of many of the maritime provinces. In 1632 a strong Dutch army joined forces with the king of Kandy to expel the Portuguese, but themselves were driven out 150 years later by a combined British and Kandian force. When the king was deposed in 1815, on account of repeated acts of cruelty and oppression, the Kandian chiefs invited General Brownrigg to take possession of the whole island, and it has since remained in British hands.

Chief Cities and Districts

Colombo, the capital, is a strongly fortified city on the south-west coast. On the opposite side of the island lies Trincomalee, described by Nelson as 'the finest harbour in the world'. Its fort is built on a peninsula connected to the mainland by a narrow isthmus protected by an almost impregnable fortress. Another strong fortress and harbour lies at Point de Galle at the very southern extremity of the island. Kandy, the ancient capital, is situated in a natural amphitheatre in the heart of the island, the city being almost surrounded by the Mahavilla Ganga river which flows into the sea not far from Trincomalee. The delightful station of Newera Ellia in the mountains south-west of Kandy has a delicious climate in which every British culinary vegetable will thrive luxuriantly. In the maritime areas, the roads pass through groves of coconut trees. The main road from Colombo to Kandy is a work of stupendous magnitude, hills having been cut away, tunnels dug, bridges built across unfordable rivers, and now has a regular mail coach. The staple products of the island are cinnamon, coffee, coconut oil, spices, precious stones and coir.

Population

The total number of inhabitants is about 1,500,000, of whom not more than 10,000 are European or descended from English, Dutch or Portuguese parents.

The Illustrations by J. Marchant, & Engraved by J. B. Allen.

The Map Drawn & Engraved by J. Rapkin.

Australia

Area and Physical Aspect

This island continent, washed on its eastern and southern shores by the Pacific, on its western and north-western shores by the Indian Ocean, has been estimated as having an area of 2,690,810 square miles, and a coastline of nearly 8,000 nautical miles. The peculiar external form of Australia may be in some degree owing to the forces to which the land is subjected by the surrounding waters, the greatest bays being formed in the south where the unbroken roll of the ocean from the pole is manifested in the Great Bight. The coastline generally is marked by deep gulfs, fine bays and capacious havens. Very few of the rivers are navigable, however, and even those that are may frequently be barred at the entrance.

Discovery

In 1536, *La Terre Australie* was supposed by geographers to be situated at the extremity of Cape Horn. In 1605 the northern coast was seen by Quiros and taken to be part of the Great South Land occupying the greater part of the Antarctic Circle. Between 1606 and 1644 the Dutch made several landings and called the island New Holland. After Cook had visited the east and north-east shores he suggested the formation of a penal colony in what is now New South Wales. The success attending this colony led to further settlements in Van Diemen's Land, Swan River, West Australia, Melbourne and Adelaide, all of which are given separate maps following this one.

Winds and Temperature

The arid and heated surface which appears to form the interior of Australia attracts the wind from the north coast and it blows to south and east in hot, violent gusts. There is no periodical recurrence of dry and rainy seasons between Cape Howe and the Tropic of Capricorn, where the variations incident to the torrid zone commence. In the north-west, however, the monsoon is accompanied by heat, thunder, lightning and heavy rains. In the southern mountains snow falls in winter and it freezes in June, July and August. Hail falls in large, irregular masses during the summer. High tide strikes almost the whole eastern coast of Australia at the same time.

Geology

The continent as a whole appears of diluvian rather than volcanic origin, although the mountain chain on the east coast has an axis of granite, with occasional large masses of greenstone basalt and other igneous rocks. In Northern Australia there is a great sandstone plateau rising to 1,800 feet above the sea and probably of palaeozoic age. The coal formation applicable for domestic or steam purposes has as yet been found only in the east coast regions. Diversity of surface and aspect produces diversity in appearance. However, the nature of vegetation is not determined by its altitude or latitude, as in other countries, but rather by the nature of the soil and the proximity to water. In many places the whole face of the country has the appearance of a landscape garden with groves, lawns and shrubberies, and it is hard to believe that such parts are uncultivated.

The Illustrations by H. Warren; & Engraved by J. Rogers.

The Map Drawn & Engraved by J. Rapkin.

New South Wales

Area and Physical Aspect

Named by Captain Cook from its fancied resemblance to the southern part of Wales in Britain, New South Wales occupies the eastern portion of Australia. Since its borders to the north and west are not yet definitely assigned, it is impossible to state its area. The general features of the surveyed districts are alternate hills and valleys, mountains and plains. A lofty ridge running almost parallel to the coast has an estimated mean altitude of 3,500 feet and is known as the Liverpool range at its northerly end, as the Blue Mountains near Sydney, and as the Australian Alps in the south. The maritime boundary is generally deeply indented and the land is bleak, barren and sometimes swampy along a belt some 5 or 6 miles wide. Beyond this coast-girdle there are forests of eucalyptus, and further inland still hills and dales of luxuriant herbiage. The rivers of Australia, even including the Murray, occupy a far less prominent geographical position than do those of any other country of similar extent, and they afford very limited communication between the coast and the interior region lying between the River Darling and the ocean. The climate generally is similar to that of southern Europe.

History

In 1787 the English government sent out a fleet of convicts to found a penal settlement at Botany Bay, then recently discovered by Captain Cook. When this bay was found to be unsuitable for the establishment of a colony, the convicts and their guards were removed to the adjacent spacious harbour Port Jackson, where the infant settlement was begun on the shores of Sydney cove in 1788. The country is now divided into 22 counties and 11 commissioners' districts.

Chief Town

Sydney, the capital, is built partly on a small promontory and partly in a narrow valley. With its large land-locked haven, it is admirably situated to be the centre of a commercial empire. The abundance of good brick earth and building stone has enabled the city to be constructed on a scale that would fairly vie with a European capital. In addition to the wharfs, stores and shipyards of the harbour, there are mills, manufactories, steam engines, breweries, etc. The inhabitants of the city and its suburbs now number between 50,000 and 60,000.

Population

The founding population in 1788 consisted of 608 male and 250 female convicts, and a guard of marines which, together with their families, numbered 212. During the following 48 years, a further 50,000 convicts were transported from England and Ireland to New South Wales, with a further 27,759 being sent to Van Diemen's Land. Transportation to New South Wales ceased in 1840. The total number of inhabitants in the colony is now over 220,000, the extent of available land being so great that for each Anglo-Saxon dwelling in the land there are more than 600 acres. The farmers keep huge flocks and herds. In 1848 there were more than 6½ million sheep, and 1¼ million horned cattle.

VICTORIA, OR PORT PHILLIP.
LOWER DARLING
NEW SOUTH WALES
SOUTH AUSTRALIA
MELBOURNE
THE GOLD DIGGINGS. Coloured
WIMMERA
WESTERN PORT
BASS' STRAIT
SCALE.
Longitude East from Greenwich
RIVER GLENELG, VICTORIA.

Victoria or Port Phillip

Area and Physical Aspect

This division of the island-continent of Australia comprises the extreme southern portion and has an estimated area of 97,000 square miles. Throughout its whole extent the district offers a great diversity of features, from the lofty alpine region in the east to the low grassy plains on its western limits. The coastline is partly formed of long stretches of unbroken beach, partly indented by bays and capacious havens. Notwithstanding the mountain chains and ridges traversing it, Victoria is remarkable for the large proportion of fertile, accessible, well-watered and comparatively level ground within its boundaries.

Rivers and Lakes

The noble river Murrumbidgee, which forms much of the northern boundary of the province, flows into the Murray and from this junction point to the sea at Lake Alexandrina. There are numerous inland lakes, whose waters are quite salt and leave large crystals to a depth of up to six inches when the extensive evaporation of the summer dries out their beds. This salt is of excellent quality and is used by squatters for all domestic purposes, requiring only to be pounded for the table.

Chief Towns

In just 12 years, Melbourne, the capital of this province has expanded from a nucleus of foliage-covered huts, with three small wooden buildings serving as church and inns, to a thriving municipality with a mayor and twelve town councillors, many stone public buildings, a markets for cattle, hay and corn, all under the superintendence of qualified inspectors, and hotels of various grades. There are churches and banks, a court-house and gaol, botanical gardens and a race-course; and a bridge is now being constructed across the Yarra-Yarra. Much of this work has been paid for by the colonists themselves and is a tribute to their enterprising spirit. Next in importance to Melbourne is Geelong, on the western shore of the bay of Port Phillip. Portland, Belfast and Alberton are rising maritime towns.

Population

The estimated number of inhabitants in Victoria for 1850 is 50,000, of whom about 15,000 live in Melbourne city. In 1846 the literate just outnumbered the illiterate amongst all age groups, but about 5,000 children are now receiving instruction.

Commerce and Industry

As in New South Wales, the most valuable and important product is wool. In 1849 total wool exports from Victoria to the United Kingdom amounted to over 12 million lbs. Two main breeds of sheep are reared: the large Leicestershire which yields 6 to 7 lbs of wool, and the Saxon or Merino breed which has a smaller carcase but much finer fleece, although it is more liable to catarrh and foot rot. Numbers of all kinds of live stock have been rising rapidly: from 1843 to 1847, the numbers of horses and horned cattle nearly trebled, and sheep increased twentyfold. Many animals are slaughtered for boiling down into tallow, lard and glue. The cultivation of the grape has been commenced and promises well. In 1848 1,300 gallons of wine and 30 of brandy were made.

PART OF SOUTH AUSTRALIA
SCALE
NOTE. The Mining Districts Col.d ♀
LAKE TORRENS
ADELAIDE.
NATIVES ON A CATAMARAN.
DINGO, OR AUSTRALIAN DOG.
SYMPRICUS.
SEAL OF SOUTH AUSTRALIA.
Gawler Range 2000 ft.
Eyre 1840
Low stony country
Plains of salsola water
Dense brush
Table topped M.
Sandy Plains
Water after rain
Barren Country with salt lakes
FLINDERS
Port Lincoln
Thistle I.
Sir J. Banks Is.
Dutton B.
Flinders Ht.
SPENCER GULF
YORK PENINSULA
Hardwicke Bay
Wooded Land
Troubridge Hill
C. Spencer
Althorpe Is.
INVESTIGATOR STRAIT
KANGAROO ISLD.
Kingscote
Nepean B.
Backstairs Pass.
Vivonne B.
C. Borda
C. Bedout
C. Couedic
C. Gantheaume
C. Willoughby
ENCOUNTER BAY
GULF OF ST. VINCENT
P. Gawler
P. Adelaide
ADELAIDE
Glenelg
Holdfast B.
Noarlunga
Aldinga B.
C. Jervis
Victor Hr.
Goolwa
Hindmarsh
L. VICTORIA
L. Albert
RUSSELL
Wellington
Gawler Tn.
STANLEY
LIGHT
GAWLER
EYRE
HINDMARSH
STURT
Mt. Barker
Macclesfield
Strathalbyn
Kapunda
Greenock
Angaston
Victoria
Barren Plains
Black Rock Hill 2750 ft.
Narrien Range
Yorke Plains
Mt. Bryan
Burra Burra
Hawdon Plains
Porcupine Hill
Mt. Remarkable
Mt. Brown visible 20 leagues
Mt. Arden
Mt. Eyre
Mt. Deception
Stony & barren plains
Overseers track
Hot Spr.
Water
Mt. Victor
Mt. Sturt
L. Gilles
Hummock Hill
Mt. Young
Middle Back Mt.
Longitude East from Greenwich

Part of South Australia

Area and Physical Aspect

The accompanying map represents only the settled portions of the colony of South Australia, an area of some 300,000 square miles which was created a province in 1834. The full extent of the colony can be seen on the general map of Australia. The distinguishing features of the province are two great inland gulfs named Spencer and St Vincent, the latter protected from the force of the ocean by Kangaroo Island. To the west of Spencer's Gulf the country is generally flat and uninteresting, while to the east and south of the Gulf of St Vincent lies a range of hills not exceeding 3,500 feet. The principal river, the Murray, rises in the Australian Alps and flows 1,200 to 1,500 before reaching Lake Victoria, an inland sea on Encounter Bay. The Torrens, on which the city of Adelaide is situated, and various other streams are almost dry for part of the year, exhibiting only a chain of ponds. The harbours are numerous, Port Lincoln being said to resemble that of Rio de Janeiro. The climate is very salubrious and offers an excellent remedial atmosphere for alleviating the diseases of Europe or Asia. Southerly winds, prevailing for most of the year, arrive cool and refreshing from the Pacific, and have an exhilarating influence.

Chief Towns

The capital of the province is Adelaide (population about 10,000), which lies on the east coast of the Gulf of St Vincent, overlooked by the Mount Lofty range. Carefully laid out, there are several pieces of land in the city reserved for ornamental purposes. The port is a secure but a barred harbour which is to be connected to the city by a railroad.

Population

In 1848, the number of people was estimated at 38,666, but by 1850 this had risen to 50,000. Perhaps one tenth of this figure are aboriginal natives.

Commerce and Industry

Throughout the province, some 36,000 acres were under cultivation in 1847, most given over to wheat, barley and oats and yielding crops sufficient to support 25 flour mills. Sheep and cattle are also reared in considerable numbers. However, the discovery of various metals in the region has altered the nature of industry in recent years, and metal ores now form the staple export. Some of the principal mines produce different kinds of copper and lead, and native gold containing a small portion of silver has also been found. At the celebrated Burra-Burra Mines in particular, copper crops out of the surface in such quantities that hundreds of tons may be removed without sinking a shaft, in the manner of quarrying rather than mining. Many persons resident in England have invested capital in the purchase of lands in South Australia, and the colony was founded according to the 'Wakefield principle' of fixing a sufficient price for the land to enable to the colony to be self-supporting. Indeed South Australia now defrays all its own expenses. The total value of exports has risen consistently over the past ten years and now stands at £446,643 per year.

The Illustrations by A. H. Wray; & Engraved by W. Lacey.

The Map, Drawn & Engraved by J. Rapkin.

Western Australia, Swan River

Area and Physical Aspect

This division of Australia has an area of about one million square miles, or more than eight times the size of the British Isles. The distinguishing feature of the colony is an elevated and occasionally steep range called the Darling Hills which runs nearly parallel with the west coast for over 400 miles, and separates the region into two distinct districts. Between the hills and the sea lies the plain of Qartania, a wooded area full of estuaries and rivers. To the east of the Darling range the country has been compared in parts to the English county of Hereford, in others to the county of Wicklow in Ireland, and in the north to Switzerland. Generally speaking, Western Australia offers a greater variety of soils than the other Australian settlements, and although there are fewer large tracts of arable land scarcely any are unavailable for some class of culture.

History

The name Swan River was first given to this portion of Western Australia by Vlaming, a Dutch navigator, who found many black swans in the neighbourhood. Public attention in England was first directed here by Captain Stirling, who reported in 1827 on the advantages of our occupying the area, and thus preventing the French from carrying out their plans to form a settlement. Accordingly in 1829 Captain Fremantle hoisted the British flag near the Swan River mouth in the name of George IV, and in 1830 grants of land were made to would-be settlers. But no proper preparation had been made, no safe anchorage ascertained, no shelter erected, no land surveyed, with the result that several ships were wrecked, survivors and their possessions were drenched in the winter rains, and altogether a quarter of a million sterling of property was destroyed. Another 15 years elapsed before boundary fences could be erected within five miles of Perth.

Chief Towns

The capital, perth, is situated about 11 miles from the sea coast on the Swan River. An unlimited supply of good water, brick-clay and timber have ensured a rapid growth in the town. Fifteen years ago building allotments were bought and sold for a bottle of grog, whereas now many are worth up to £1,000; and the town has churches of different Christian denominations, a government house, a bank, gaol, hospital, hotels and so on. Fremantle, the sea-port of Perth, is built entirely of white limestone which dazzles the visitor in summer. During the winter season, bay whaling is carried on.

Population

The European inhabitants numbered 4,622 in 1848, but there is abundant space for an extension of the population and convicts are to be sent to Western Australia to improve the harbours, open roads, cut down forests and prepare the colony for free settlers. The regularity of the seasons and the fineness of climate enable settlers to grow many of the vegetable plants associated with southern Europe, including vines, olives and citrus fruits. Predominantly a country of sheep-rearing, the colony exported 301,965 lbs of wool in 1849 from its 141,123 sheep.

VAN DIEMEN'S ISLAND
OR
TASMANIA
HOBART TOWN.
RESIDENCE OF THE V. D. L. COMPANY'S AGENT, CIRCULAR HEAD.
THYLACINUS CYNOCEPHALUS.
SCALE
Miles
Longitude East from Greenwich
BASS' STRAIT
BANKS' STRAIT
FURNEAUX
ISLANDS
FLINDERS I.
BARREN I.
INDIAN OCEAN
SOUTH PACIFIC OCEAN
DEVON
DORSET
CORNWALL
WESTMORLAND
SOMERSET
GLAMORGAN
CUMBERLAND
MONMOUTH
PEMBROKE
BUCKINGHAM
KENT
HOBARTON
Launceston
Campbelltown
Oatlands
Bothwell
Hamilton
New Norfolk
Brighton
Richmond
Sorell
Ross
Perth
Westbury
Longford
Fingal
WOOLNORTH
HAMPSHIRE HILLS
SURREY HILLS
MIDDLESEX PLAINS
TASMAN PEN.
Port Arthur
Maria I.
OYSTER BAY
Bay of Fires
Macquarie Harb.
PORT DAVEY
S. West C.
South C.
Tasman Hd.
De Witts or Maatsuyker I.
Frankland Range
Eldon Range
Great L.
Three Hummock I.
Hunter I.
Robbins I.
Albatros I.
Circular Hd.
Port Sorell
PORT DALRYMPLE
George Tn.
Waterhouse I.
C. Portland
Swan I.
Clark I.
Preservation I.

Van Diemen's Land or Tasmania

Area and Physical Aspect

Situated at the south-east extremity of Australia, this fine island comprises an area of more than 15,000,000 acres. Its lofty wooded mountains are very picturesque, the tallest being Mount Humboldt (5,520 feet); while the extensive plains are extremely fertile. The northern shores present a line of low sandy beaches, broken by rocky headlands on which the surf breaks with great violence, the other portions of the coast being mostly rocky but abounding in good harbours.

History

The famous navigator Tasman, who first visited the southern shores in 1642, named the island after Van Diemen, then governor-general of the Dutch East Indies, although he did not suspect its insularity. Formal possession of Tasmania was taken in 1803 by Lieutenant Bowen, sent there from New South Wales to form a penal settlement, and in 1819 free emigration was sanctioned. The island was given a separate government from New South Wales in 1825, and has its own lieutenant-governor aided by an executive and legislative council.

Chief Towns

Hobart Town, the capital (population over 21,000), occupies a commanding position on the River Derwent about 20 miles from the sea. Its streets are wide and long and several have been macadamized. Many of the public buildings, including a cathedral, court, hospital and government houses, are commodious and well-built. A rivulet running through the centre of town supplies water for drinking and for turning timber and corn mills. Launceston, the second town, is less imposing, but its position at the head of a navigable portion of the river Tamar in the north of the island has made it an important trading centre, the river being accessible to vessels of 500 tons burthen. A good road extends between these two towns as far as Oatlands. The most highly cultivated district in the island is Norfolk Plains, south of Launceston.

Population

The aborigines have all perished or been removed from the island. In 1848 the white population was said to be about 70,000, of whom 20,449 were convicts under transportation, some being employed by the government, others assigned to private individuals.

Commerce and Industry

The staple products are wool, grain, cattle and sheep. The seas abound in whales and the shore with shell-fish. Oysters, once plentiful, are said to have become almost extinct. Coal is supposed to exist in several places, but principally at Port Arthur. There are numerous marble quarries. Most of the trade is conducted with England, which received about two-thirds of Tasmania's exports in 1847.

Vegetable and Animal Kingdom

The island has a wide variety of trees, the gum being the largest, though several others are adapted for ship and house building. Among the most picturesque are the black and silver wattle, from which tanning acid is obtained. Nearly all the trees are evergreen, growing tall and straight. There are many birds and marsupial animals of the kind found in Australia, and a panther-like dog of formidable size which commits dreadful havoc among the settlers' flocks, though it flies from man.

The Illustrations by H. Warren & Engraved by J.B. Allen.

The Map Drawn & Engraved by J. Rapkin.

New Zealand

Area and Physical Aspect

This extensive and valuable group is 13,000 miles from England and 16,500 miles from the east coast of the USA and forms the Antipodes. The three principal islands have a total estimated area of between 80,000 and 122,000 square miles. The Northern Island, also called New Ulster, has a chain of high mountains, some as much as 14,000 feet in height, forming a central back-bone. Up to the level of perpetual snow, the whole mass is covered with lofty timber and vegetation, intersected by various streams and cascades. The Middle Island, New Munster, has extensive grassy plains, suitable for cultivation; while the Southern Island, sometimes called New Leinster or Stewart's Island, has been little explored. Igneous in origin, the country has several active volcanoes and there are places where boiling water is found within a few feet of the surface. Mount Egmont, near the entrance of Cook's Straits, forms an immense volcanic cone visible at a distance of 85 miles.

History

A part of one of the islands was discovered by the Dutch navigator Tasman in 1642, but little further explored until Captain Cook visited the North Island in 1769 and took nominal possession for his sovereign. After this period the islands were frequently visited by whaling ships and became a refuge for runaway convicts from Australia. In 1839 the New Zealand Company
commenced a systematic effort for the occupation of the Northern Island. Up to July 1849, the total quantity of land granted through the Surveying Department has been over 5 million acres, of which 274,000 acres in the Auckland District alone. For the purposes of government the islands are divided into two separate provinces with a governor-in-chief over the whole residing in Auckland.

Chief Towns and Harbours

In 1848 there were nine principal European settlements in New Zealand, the most important being Auckland and Wellington in the North Island, and Otago and Nelson on the Middle Island, although it is proposed to found the Canterbury Settlement at Port Cooper, also on the Middle Island. Scattered over a wide distance, these settlements have poor communication with each other, even for persons on horseback. Auckland, the capital, has a population of about 3,500 and is situated in open country offering a large extent of arable land and a harbour nearby, The Bay of Islands to the north has deep water close to the shore and excellent anchorage, as does Port Tauranga on the bay of Plenty. Cook's Straits, which separate the two main islands, abound in good harbours, but the weather is said to be tempestuous and uncertain. Port Nicholson, on which the town of Wellington is situated, is perfectly sheltered.

Population

The number of British settlers in the three islands, including some Americans, Germans and French, is about 20,000, while the natives are estimated at 107,265. The natives are well armed with rifles and double-barrelled guns and have been engaged in serious contests with the English, chiefly on account of land. There are three Christian missions employed in the conversion of the aborigines.

The Illustrations by H. Winkles & Engraved by T. Wrightson.

The Map Drawn & Engraved by J. Rapkin.

Polynesia, or Islands in the Pacific

A large part of the Pacific Ocean between the Tropics of Cancer and Capricorn is studded with islands of all sizes, some volcanic, some coralline, some isolated, some in groups. European knowledge of these islands has been acquired by several distinguished navigators, including Mendana, De Torres, Tasman, Bougainville and Captain Cook. Nevertheless, all islands in the Pacific (except the Marquesas, claimed by the French) remain in the quiet possession of their aboriginal inhabitants. Many enjoy luxuriant vegetation with wild fruits unknown to Europeans, and are thickly peopled. There is no space here to provide more than brief allusions to the principal groups.

SANDWICH ISLANDS are ten in number, the largest being Owyhee or Hawaii, with an area of 4,000 square miles, and a population of about 10,000. Mountainous, with several volcanic peaks, they are much frequented by whaling vessels.

THE MARIAN AND LADRONES and the CAROLINE ISLANDS are said to resemble the Phillippines, but are little known.

NEW BRITAIN, NEW IRELAND and NEW HANOVER are not fully explored. Low and thickly wooded with a central chain of volcanic mountains, they are well peopled by a race who move about in canoes 90 feet long, formed out of a single tree.

SOLOMON ISLANDS are peopled by a black race who go entirely naked and live in a state of continual warfare. The country is covered in dense vegetation.

THE NEW HEBRIDES were named by Cook in 1774. The largest was supposed by Quiros in 1606 to be part of a great southern continent. Pigs and poultry abound; yams grow to a great size, sometimes weighing 50 lbs.

NEW CALEDONIA is in general mountainous, with a bleak and barren appearance. The native language is totally unlike any other spoken in the Pacific islands.

THE FRIENDLY ISLANDS are low and highly cultivated. Tongataboo is the chief island and thickly peopled. Almost every person is missing the little finger of one or both hands, which indicates grief for some deceased person. Idolatry and cannibalism prevail. The Tonga Islands present similar features.

HERVEY ISLANDS are of difficult access owing to coral reefs. They are richly cultivated, and in Roratonga, where there are 7,000 inhabitants, the majority have embraced Christianity.

THE MARQUESAS have a rugged aspect. The land is high and of volcanic origin.

THE SOCIETY ISLANDS were so named by Captain Cook in honour of the Royal Society. They form an extensive group of magnificent scenery, with fertile soil and luxuriant vegetation. Otaheite, the principal island, has about 10,000 inhabitants.

PITCAIRN'S ISLAND was peopled by the English seamen who mutinied in HMS Bounty and landed here with their Otaheitean wives. Though the soil is rich and the climate delightful, it is difficult to make land, even in a small boat.

NORFOLK ISLAND has for several years been the penal settlement of New South Wales and Van Diemen's Island. Ridged by steep hills, it is known for the celebrated pine (*aurucaria excelsa*) which grows to 200 feet high.

AFRICA.
ARAB FAMILY OF ALGERIA
BEDOUIN ARABS ENCAMPMENT
BOSJESMAN HOTTENTOTS
WILD BUSHMEN
St. HELENA
KORRANNA HOTTENTOTS
NORTH
ATLANTIC
OCEAN
SOUTH
ATLANTIC
OCEAN
INDIAN
OCEAN
ARABIAN
SEA
PERSIAN GULF
SEA OF OMAN
GULF OF GUINEA
SPAIN
ASIA MINOR
AZORES OR WESTERN Is.
CANARIES
CAPE VERD Is.
MADEIRA
Sardinia
Sicily
Candia
Cyprus
Jerusalem
Suez
Medina
Mecca
Mocha
Aden
Socotra
Tropic of Cancer
Equator
Tropic of Capricorn
Mountains of the Moon
The Great Marsh
Ascension
St. Helena
Seychelles
Amirante Is.
Mauritius or I. of France
Bourbon I.
Rodrigue
Cargados
Delagoa B.
Port Natal & D'Urban
CAPE OF GOOD HOPE
C. Lagulhas
Lagulhas Bank
St. Helena B.
Walvisch B.
Port Alexander
Philip de Benguela
S. Paul de Loando
C. Delgado
Quiloa
Zanzibar
Mombaz
Melinda Port
C. Guardafui
Ras Hafoun
SEA OF BAB EL MANDEB
Bight of Biafra
Fernando Po
Is. St. Thomas
Annobon I.
C. Blanco
C. Verd
Bijouga or Bissagos Is.
Bathurst
Str. of Gibraltar
Khartoum
Dongola
LOANGO
CONGO
ANGOLA
BENGUELA
MOZAMBIQUE
MOZAMBIQUE CHANNEL
SCALE
Longitude West 20 from Greenwich
Longitude East 40 from Greenwich

Africa

Area and Physical Aspect

The area of this great continent has been variously estimated by the geographers Malte Brun and Ukert at 13,430,000 and 11,961,675 square miles. More than five-sixths of the region are still unknown to European geographers, although it may be possible to cross westwards from Sofola with the aid of Moorish traders who travel in caravans. The unexplored interior is supposed to be a great plateau rising in successive steps from the south.

Mountains and Deserts

The Atlas Mountains extend along the north coast, reaching their greatest altitude at 13,200 feet in Morocco. The Egyptian mountains of Magarah and Mocattham are much smaller and run along the west bank of the Nile, a branch of the Lybian chain. Abyssinia is an alpine district whose peaks are covered with perpetual snow even in the Torrid Zone. On the east coast there appears to be a continuous chain of mountains terminating in Table Mountain at the extreme south. A further chain seems to run up the west coast. Whether these north-south chains are connected to others running east to west has never been ascertained. Of the alleged Mountains of the Moon we know nothing. Vast sandy wastes with occasional green and habitable spots characterize Africa. The Sahara is said to stretch 2,600 from east to west with a breadth of 750 miles. The scorching winds, intense sunlight and suffocating sandstorms there are fatal to animal and vegetable life.

Rivers and Lakes

The chief streams of which we have any definite and accredited account are the Nile, Niger, Joliba, Senegal, Gambia, Congo, Orange, Quilimane and the Haines. The Nile rises in Abyssinia and enters the Mediterranean at Rosetta. The Niger has its source in the Kong Mountains and enters the Atlantic after 1,660 miles. Charting its course has cost many British lives. The Senegal and the Gambia also flow into the Atlantic and are navigable for some distance. The Orange River in South Africa sometimes ceases to flow in the dry season. Of the Congo, Quilimane and Haines little is known. The only large lake yet charted is the Tchad, although it is said that there is another 300 miles long on the east coast about the 10th parallel.

Population

Calculations of numbers are founded on very vague premises, and the total could be between 100 and 150 million. All the native peoples are negroes of different shades or the descendants of Arabs, Moors and Berbers migrated from Asia. In the known parts of Africa alone 150 languages are spoken. Christianity is said to have been extensively diffused in Africa during the second century AD but was supplanted by Islamism, which is also taking over in parts from the image-worship of the negroes.

Commerce

Africa is rich in various products and but for the slave trade the mercantile intercourse with Europe would now have been considerably augmented. Gold, ivory, various gums, spices, drugs and so on are widely obtainable and are exchanged for cloth, hardware, muskets and rum from England and France.

CAPE COLONY
ENTRANCE TO THE KNYSNA
GRAHAM'S TOWN
CAPE TOWN
HOTTENTOTS
KAFFRARIA
LITTLE NAMAQUA LAND
Extensive Desert Plains
Koranas
Orange River
Gariep or Orange R.
Griqua T.n or Klaarwater
Pella
Desolate Plains
Onder Roggeveld
Onder Bokkeveld
Mid Roggeveld
Kl. Roggeveld
Bokkeveld Karroo
Clanwilliam
Tulbagh
Worcester
Paarl
Stellenbosch
Caledon
Swellendam
George
Mossel B.
Plettenberg B.
Uitenhage
Graaff Reynet
Camdeboo
Beaufort
Somerset
Grahams T.n
Bathurst
Albany
Algoa Bay
Saldanha Bay
St. Helena Bay
Table Bay
Cape Town
Constantia
False Bay
Cape of Good Hope
C. Agulhas
Stormberg
Winterberg
Zwart Ruggen
Groote Zwart B.
Kannaland
Elephants R.
Longitude East from 22 Greenwich
SCALE
Miles

Cape Colony

Area and Physical Aspect

This extensive British possession covers an area of some 200,000 square miles at the southern extremity of the African continent. Generally composed of chains of lofty mountains and intervening plains and valleys, running east to west, with the exception of one range stretching northward along the western coast for about 250 miles. Between the Zwart Bergen, or Black Mountains, and the Nieuwveld's Bergen lies the Great Karroo, a desert land 1,000 feet above the sea. Towards the southern extremity are several peaks, of which the highest are Table Mountain (3,582 feet), Devil's Peak (3,315 feet) and Lion's Head (2,760 feet). The largest river is the Orange or Gariep, other streams being much smaller. The climate is very salubrious, the summer heat of the coast being mitigated by constant breezes.

History

Ten years after its initial discovery by Bartholomew Diaz in 1487, the Cape of Good Hope was finally rounded by Vasco da Gama. From that time the Cape continued to be a temporary rendezvous of European mariners for more than a century and ships sailing to India would bury dispatches there for homebound vessels to carry back. No settlement was formed until 1650, when the Dutch landed 100 men and 100 women from Amsterdam. It has been in British possession since captured from the French in 1806.

Chief Towns and Harbours

Cape Town, which stands at the foot of Table Mountain, is clean and well laid out, with strong fortifications nearby, capable of resisting any force. There are few good havens. Table Bay, on whose shores Cape Town is built is exposed to heavy surf when the wind blows from the north-east, although the anchorage could be made secure by the construction of a break-water. The royal navy has a station and dockyard at Simon's Bay. Other harbours are mostly restricted to small vessels.

Population

The total inhabitants were estimated in 1846 at 185,000, of whom 80,580 are white and the rest coloured. The religion of the majority of Christians is that of the Dutch Reformed Church, and there is also a large proportion of Mohamedans throughout the population as a whole.

Animal Kingdom

The largest and the smallest of the animal kingdom are found in South Africa, from the elephant weighing 4,000 lbs to the black streaked mouse weighing one quarter of an ounce; and from the ostrich, 6 feet high, to the creeper bird, which is about the size of a cherry. There are many kinds of antelope, also lions, hyenas, zebras, and that singular animal the gnu. Monkeys of all sizes are found in the mountains.

Commerce and Industry

Provisions of all kinds are cheap to buy, with beef at about 1 1/4*d.* per pound. Wine and brandy are made in every district. Sheep, cattle and horses all arrive at a large size. The staple products are corn, wool, wine, timber, hides, etc. Total exports in 1849 amounted to £245,984. Steam navigation has now brought the colony within little more than one month's sail from England.

The Illustrations by H. Winkles & Engraved by W. Lacey

The Map Drawn & Engraved by J. Rapkin

Natal and Kaffraria

Area and Physical Aspect

This recently established British colony covers an area of about 16,000 square miles, but the political boundaries are ill-defined. The country consists mainly of undulating plains, with numerous table-lands, cut through by rivers rising in the higher districts and generally flowing an easterly course towards the ocean. The chain of mountains bounding the colony is divisible into two, the Great and Little Draakberg, the former having an average altitude of 5,000 feet above the sea. The area of Independent Kaffraria to the south of Natal is under the dominion of the native chiefs, supervised by the governor of the Cape colony. The Zulu Country to the north east is little known.

Rivers

Some of the rivers require special notice. The Umzinckulu separates the north-east from the south-west parts of the colony and flows through magnificent forest scenery, The Omganie river is about 15 yards wide at nearly 2 miles from its mouth. The Tugela rises in the Snowy Mountains about 250 miles from the coast. All these streams have very sweet and translucent water.

Climate

Although generally warm, the climate is salubrious, with clear skies, and refreshing rains for much of the year. Hot winds are rare, and the influence of the trade winds means that there are few extreme fluctuations.

Chief Towns

The principal harbour is Port Natal, where the entrance to the haven is about 300 yards wide and 12 feet deep at high water. It is proposed to deepen the port by dredging. Pieter Maritzburg, the capital, about 50 miles from Port Natal, is a large well-watered city, and centre of an active internal traffic. The population is now between 1,500 and 2,000, but many of the Dutch Boers who were its most valuable citizens have migrated into the interior.

Districts

The colony is divided into 11 districts, many of which provide fine land for grazing or other agricultural purposes. Dutch farmers have reared sheep and cattle with some success in Impafane, Umvoti, Upper Tukela and Umzinyati. Coal is found in abundance in several districts and much of the land is well-suited to the cultivation of cotton, tobacco and maize. D'Urban will sustain a dense population. Sugar, indigo, cotton, coffee and beans all grow well here. Many of the inland areas have luxuriant vegetation and produce tropical fruits.

Population

The number of white colonists is not accurately ascertained but is probably upwards of 5,000. The native population is estimated at 120,000, but the demand for labour is likely to cause immigration of large numbers of Zoolas and others from the adjacent regions. The obtainment of a passage from Europe and 20 acres of land for each emigrant for the trifling sum of £10 is likely to cause a large increase in the white population.

Commerce

In addition to wool and cotton, ivory is also exported in large quantities. Recently, as the Dutch have left the colony, exports have declined from £15,146 in 1847 to £10,866 in 1849; while imports increased by over £5,000 in the same period.

The Illustrations by H. Winkles; & Engraved by E. Radclyffe.

The Map, Drawn & Engraved by J. Rankin.

Western Africa

The regions of Africa shown on the accompanying map are generally known as Senegambia and Guinea, these being divided into smaller areas.

SENEGAMBIA consists of several states or kingdoms, including various French and British settlements at Fort St Louis, Goree, Bathurst and others. The coast line is flat and thickly wooded, with three great rivers, the Senegal, the Gambia and the Rio Grande entering the Atlantic. The climate is almost insupportable to Europeans at all times of the year, being very hot and humid. Further inland the country becomes elevated into parallel mountain terraces increasing in height towards the south, and here the climate is more salubrious.

GUINEA has been assigned various limits by different nations. The accompanying map includes the country between Cape Verga and the Bight of Biafra. The general aspect of the Atlantic frontier is one of immense forests, with lofty backgrounds clothed in underwood, although there are several tracts of sandy, sterile coastland with chains of lagoons.

Beginning with the north coast, the British staate of Sierra Leone was made a free settlement for liberated negroes in 1787. The population of about 50,000 are distributed in villages, apart from the capital, Freetown, which is overlooked by a fort containing 10,000 inhabitants.

The Grain Coast, extending for about 300 miles, also includes a settlement for liberated slaves, termed Liberia. The Ivory Coast forms a slightly curved line of about 300 miles from west to east. It contains no important towns or rivers, but the country is populous and the people said to be more violent than those in any other part of Africa. A further 350 miles is covered by the Gold Coast, which includes the territories of the Ashantees, Fantees, and other powerful nations. On this coast England has recently purchased Christianborg and other old Danish forts, together with sovereign rights over nearly 200 miles and command of the Volta river. There are further commanding military positions at Cape Coast Castle and Accra. The Slave Coast extends from the Volta to the Lagos rivers and includes the populous kingdoms Kobo, Quitta, Popo, Ardrak and Whidah. In Benin the great river Niger flows into the sea after a distance of 2,300 from its source in the Kong Mountains.

Behind the above named eoasts lie fertile and thickly peopled territories. The most powerful and civilized nation are the Ashantees, numbering about 1,000,000 with a further 3,000,000 vassals. The capital, Komassi, is only one of many populous towns in this monarchy, said to have been founded in 1700 AD. Dahomey, to the east of Ashantee, is also a powerful kingdom, whose despotic monarch is the greatest slave-dealer in Africa. The country drained by the Niger, Becroft and Calabar rivers is fertile. Little is known of the kingdoms further inland.

Efforts are being made to expand trade with West Africa, in order to atone for the injuries that European nations have inflicted. Not only have 100 million Africans been deported as slaves by nominally Christian nations, but the trade itself has provoked constant warfare among the Africans.

The Illustrations by H. Winkles; & Engraved by G. Greatbach.

The Map, Drawn & Engraved by J. Rapkin.

Northern Africa

This extensive region, under the designation Barbary, stretches about 2,600 miles along the Atlantic and Mediterranean coasts, Known to the Phoenicians in 1,000 BC, and centre of the Carthagianian empire, it was subsequently conquered by the Romans, who divided it into five provinces. On the decline of Saracenic power in Spain the Moors withdrew and the Turks formed the maritime states of Barbary which, for centuries, harassed the Christian nations of Europe.

TUNIS extends for about 500 miles along the Mediterranean coast with a cultivated region stretching 200 to 300 miles into the interior. Well watered by numerous streams, the irrigated areas are fertile and productive, and the mountains contain mines of silver, copper and lead. The capital, Tunis, is about 10 miles from the site of ancient Carthage,and has a population of 130,000. Goletta, the citadel and harbour of Tunis, is strongly fortified. The country is governed by a viceroy appointed by the Turkish empire, although the army and several districts have their own chiefs.

ALGIERS lies along the coast of the south-western Mediterranean. Having passed through the hands of the Romans, Goths, Vandals, Greeks and Saracens, Algeria was successfully invaded in the sixteenth century by the Spaniards, who were expelled in their turn by a pirate named Barbarossa. Under his rule, the country became a centre for attacks on Christian vessels and the enslavement of Christian prisoners, These atrocities continued for about 200 years, despite opposition from the French, English and Venetians. In 1830 The French invaded with a large army and, after heavy losses, gained control of the country. The population was estimated in 1840 at about 30,000, of whom 7,000 were French troops, the rest Moors, Negroes and other foreigners. There are several rivers, though none of great size and some lakes. The ridges of mountains reach a considerable elevation in certain parts. The city of Algiers is built on the side of a hill rising gradually from the shore and has an imposing effect from its fortresses, mosques and castles.

MOROCCO, with a total area of about 300,000 square miles, is divided into four regions: Fez in the north, Morocco in the centre, Tafilet in the east and Suz in the south. After the retreat of the Moor in the twelfth century, the country became part of the Mogreb, or 'great empire of the west' of the Berbers. The present ruling family has reigned for 300 years, and the emperor is entirely despotic, his power supported by Negro mercenaries and a large Moorish army. His body guard alone number 6,000 troops. Little is known of the topography of Morocco. The Atlas mountains traverse the country, and from them flow numerous streams, though none of great magnitude. There are few good harbours, the principal port Mogadore being formed by a small island. Tangier is the residence of the European consuls. The capital, Morocco, stands in the centre of a great plain and is fortified in the ancient style. Estimates of the total population vary widely between 2 and 14 million.

The Illustrations by J. Marchant & Engraved by J. B. Allen.

The Map, Drawn & Engraved by J. Rapkin.

Egypt and Arabia Petraea

AREA AND PHYSICAL ASPECT

This celebrated region, famed in both ancient and modern times, has had its limits frequently altered by conquests and is vaguely defined by geographers. The area is variously estimated at from 140,000 to 200,000 square miles, with a cultivable surface of less than 20,000 square miles. The country is divided into three areas: Lower Egypt, which is flat and much intersected by branches of the Nile; Central Egypt, a region of sandstone hills; and Upper Egypt, more elevated with granite ridges and many oases in the midst of desert. The climate is warm, with the most pleasant periods being the spring in Lower Egypt and the autumn and winter in Upper and Central Egypt. Except near the sea shore, very little rain falls.

RIVERS

The Nile is nearly 2,000 miles long but seldom a mile broad except when it overflows its banks. It rises in Abyssinia, and swollen by molten snows from the highlands and by its adjacent tributaries reaches its highest between June and October. The rich deposit left when the waters recede and the fertilization caused by irrigation render the period of inundation of great moment to the Egyptians.

HISTORY

At its greatest the ancient empire of Sesostris Rhames, who supposedly lived at the same time as Moses, is said to have extended as far as the Ganges in India, Libya and Ethiopia. Later conquered by the Persians, Greeks (it was Alexander who founded Alexandria), and Romans, Egypt fell to the followers of the Crescent during the rapid spread of Mahomedanism and remained in the hands of a succession of Saladin princes for several centuries. The Mamelukes held sway for nearly five centuries, until defeated by Napoleon 1798. The French then capitulated to a combined Anglo-Indian army in 1803. Mahomed Ali Pacha, who was then made viceroy for the Ottoman Porte, was an able, ambitious and unscrupulous man who undertook many useful reforms in Egypt, building up a large fleet and army and considerable commerce. The present ruler, although nominally under Turkish sovereignty, is really independent. He is aided by a council who are generally chosen from among the governors of the provinces. In the villages there are local chiefs, or sheiks, invested with considerable authority.

CHIEF CITIES

Cairo, the capital, has a magnificent mosque and palace built by Mahomed Ali, though the streets are generally narrow. It is more oriental than Alexandria, a strongly fortified and well-situated trading city on the Mediterranean coast.

POPULATION

Of the total of nearly 2,000,000 people, the great majority are Arab Egyptians, the remainder being Copts, Turks, wandering Arabians, white and Negro slaves, Nubians, etc. Although numbering only about 20,000 the Turks are the dominant race and constitute the aristocracy. The Fellahs, who are the agricultural and general labourers, live in very wretched and degraded conditions. The Bedouins, who are the principal owners of camels, have abandoned their former predatory life and are now charged with the conveyance of Anglo-Indian mails and baggage from Alexandria to Suez.

The Illustrations by J. Marchant & Engraved by J. Rogers.

The Map Drawn & Engraved by J. Rapkin.

North America

Area and Physical Aspect

Separated from the southern part of the continent by the Isthmus of Panama, in places not more than 40 miles wide, North America is about 4,500 miles in length from north to south, and is marked along its eastern shores by the great inland seas and gulfs of Hudson, Baffin, St Lawrence and Mexico. It is rich in coal, iron and copper, and the gold region of California seems inexhaustible. Although the voyages of the European navigators, from Cabot to Captain Cook, have now traced almost all points of the coastline, some parts of the far north remain to be discovered.

Mountains and Plains

The most marked feature is the vast range of the Rocky Mountains running parallel to the Pacific down the west side, In the east the Apalachian Mountains also run north to south from Canada to Georgia in the United States. There are three great lowlands: the Mississippi basin, the western plain between the Rocky Mountains and the Pacific, and the eastern lowlands between the Apalachians and the Atlantic. The general dip of the land is from north to south throughout the United States.

Rivers and Lakes

The chief rivers are the Missouri and Mississippi, which together run 4,424 miles from source to mouth, and the St Lawrence. The lakes of North America are the largest in the world, the five great lakes of Superior, Huron, Michigan, Erie and Ontario reaching depths of 500 to 1,000 feet.

Vegetable and Animal Kingdom

Only a small number of plant species are identical with the vegetation of Europe, Asia or Africa. All kinds of bread corn grow as far north as 58° of latitude. The potato is indigenous to the continent. Many kinds of timber tree, including pine, cedar, oak, maple and walnut form large forests. There are few large quadrupeds among the native animals, although the polar and black bear are found in the north and there are great herds of deer, cariboo, bison and buffalo further south. Many of the birds have splendid plumage but no song. Serpents abound, and the rattle-snake is peculiar to America.

Population

When the first Europeans arrived, America was comparatively densely peopled by a copper-coloured race who ranged the country from Hudson's Bay to Panama. The Arctic coasts were the abode of a different people, the Esquimaux. At the beginning of the sixteenth century there were probably 25,000,000 aboriginal peoples; but this number has now been reduced to about 3,000,000 and in another century they may have nearly ceased to exist. War against the conquerors, the destruction of hunting grounds and the introduction of disease have all tended towards the rapid extermination of a fine race. In Central America the Spaniards additionally deported many Indians to work in the mines and plantations of other parts of America. At the present time the total number of inhabitants from Hudson's Bay to Panama probably does not exceed 32,000,000, of whom about 20,000,000 are of pure European blood, the rest being Indians, Negro slaves and people of mixed race.

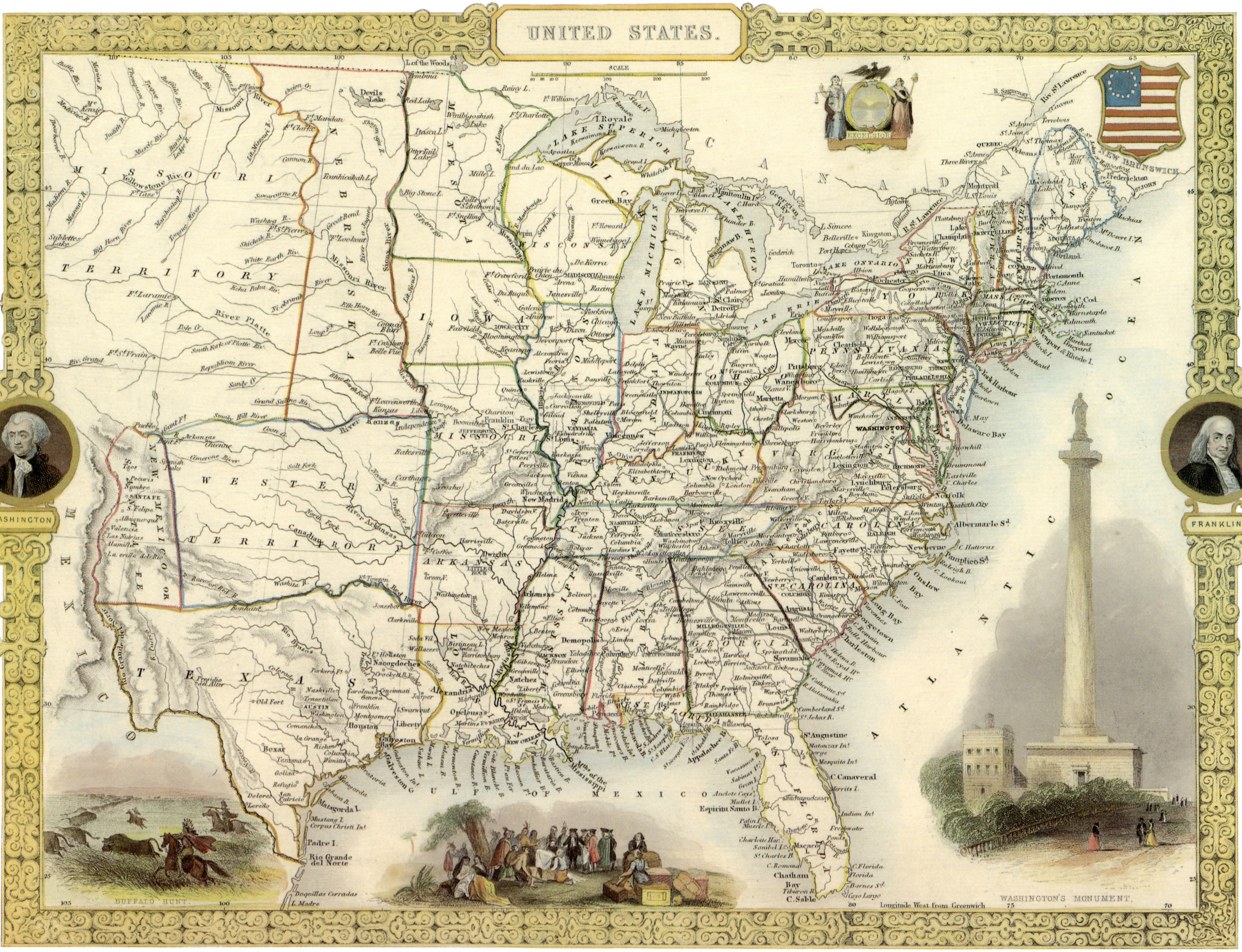

UNITED STATES.
FRANKLIN
WASHINGTON
WASHINGTON'S MONUMENT
BUFFALO HUNT
Longitude West from Greenwich
SCALE
ATLANTIC OCEAN
GULF OF MEXICO
MEXICO
CANADA
LAKE SUPERIOR
LAKE MICHIGAN
LAKE HURON
LAKE ERIE
LAKE ONTARIO
MISSOURI TERRITORY
NEBRASKA
WESTERN TERRITORY
NEW MEXICO OR SANTA FE
TEXAS
ARKANSAS
IOWA
MINESOTA
WISCONSIN
MICHIGAN
ILLINOIS
INDIANA
OHIO
KENTUCKY
TENNESSEE
MISSISSIPPI
ALABAMA
GEORGIA
FLORIDA
LOUISIANA
MISSOURI
PENNSYLVANIA
NEW YORK
VIRGINIA
NORTH CAROLINA
SOUTH CAROLINA
MAINE
WASHINGTON
NEW BRUNSWICK

United States

Area and Physical Aspect

It is obviously impossible to describe the physical aspect of so vast a country (1,300,000 square miles) in any detail in a limited space, but a few general statistics may assist in illustrating the chief points. Generally speaking the United States territories consist of extensive natural forests, interspersed with open plains termed prairies. The whole country is well watered and presents considerable variety of soil and climate. The longest rivers are the Missouri, the Mississippi and the Arkansas, and even the smaller rivers are navigable for many miles for sloops, etc. Many of the principal mountains are over 4,000 feet high, and Mount Washington in New Hampshire is 6,230 feet. The climate is, of course, influenced by the degree of distance from the equator, but it is much colder in North America than in the same latitude in Europe.

History

Whether America was known to the ancients is a subject of dispute among scholars, although it is highly probable that the Northmen of Europe landed there five centuries before the discoveries of Columbus. A Runic inscription still exists in Naraghansett Bay. After the voyages of Columbus and Cabot in 1492 and 1497, Spain devoted its attentions to developing the central and southern portions of America, while Queen Elizabeth directed the resources of England to the north. After early failures several colonies were formed on various parts of the coast, either by enterprising individuals or by associations both religious and commercial. Apart from the English, the Dutch, Swedes, Finns and other Europeans also formed settlements. In 1776 the thirteen colonies declared their independence and constituted themselves the United States of America, since which time several other states have been added, the total now numbering 26 states and 5 territories.

Population

During the 50 years from 1790 to 1840 the population increased over four-fold and it is estimated that the total is now probably 25,000,000, with a further 313,000 Indians living mostly between the Mississippi and the area west of the Rocky Mountains. The largest concentrations of people live in the eastern states. Altogether there are around 400,000 free coloured people and great numbers of slaves, most of them in the southern states. In 1850 Virginia alone had 473,972 slaves, South Carolina, 384,720, and their numbers are still increasing. In 1840 the proportion of free persons to 1 slave throughout all the states was 5.86, and Massachusetts, Maine, Vermont and Michigan were the only states without slaves. There is no state religion and all forms of Christian worship are protected. Generally speaking the people are religious, but much split into sects.

Government

Each state has its own constitution, executive and legislative department and a governor who is elected in some cases by the people, in others by the legislature. The central Congress, which has its seat at Washington, consists of two houses and a President. The members of the two houses are representatives of the states. In the eastern and middle states the suffrage is almost universal, and throughout the Union voting by ballot prevails.

MEXICO,
CALIFORNIA AND TEXAS.
RUINS AT UXMAL, YUCATAN.
GOLD WASHING.
MEXICAN PEASANTRY.
NORTH PACIFIC OCEAN
GULF OF MEXICO
CAMPECHE BAY
HONDURAS BAY
OREGON
GREAT INTERIOR BASIN OF CALIFORNIA
NEW OR UPPER CALIFORNIA
UNITED STATES
TEXAS
NEW MEXICO
LUIS POTOSI
ZACATECAS
VALLADOLID
Tropic of Cancer
The newly discovered GOLD districts.
Coloured thus
SCALE
Longitude West 105 from Greenwich
The Illustrations by H. Warren & Engraved by J. Rogers.
The Map Drawn & Engraved by J. Rapkin.

Mexico, California and Texas

The descriptions of Mexico, Texas and Yucatan must be reserved for other numbers of the Atlas. We shall here confine ourselves to Upper, or New California.

Area and Physical Aspect

Upper or New California covers an area of about 350,000 square miles. Three mountain ranges, the Monterey Ridge, the Sierra Nevada range and the Wahsatch or Colorado Ridge divide the country into three districts. The largest of these, a table land some 4,000-5,000 feet above the sea, is a desert covered with the fragments of quartz and volcanic matter washed from the mountains. Indeed the character of the whole country is evidently volcanic. To the north there are many boiling springs of sulphur, salt, magnesia, and warm mud lakes. The mountain torrents carry down large quantities of granitic formations in which great mineral wealth will probably be discovered. Although New Helvetia and Francisco Plain have large and rich tracts for cultivation, the general aspect of the country is not so favourable for tillage as for pasturage, which furnishes provender for herds of wild cattle, horses, deer and various animals. Three main rivers, the Colorado, the St Joachim and the Sacramento, are fed by numerous tributaries. The Sacramento is navigable for 50 miles for ships, and 150 for boats, and small steamers have now been sent there from the United States.

Climate

Like other places on the west coast of America extreme temperatures prevail; there are blustering winds on the coast and intense heat in the interior, with sudden blasts of air from the snow-clad mountains, which bring on remittent fevers.

History

Discovered by a Spaniard in 1544, the country was later visited by Sir Francis Drake, to whom the Indians chiefs gave sovereignty for England. In 1822, when Mexico declared itself a republic, California was added to its territories, and after several revolutions and plots it was ceded to the United States in 1848.

Chief Towns

The capital, San Franciso, stands on one of the finest natural harbours in the world, which would hold all the shipping of England. In 1841 the town was almost in ruins, but now its population numbers about 5,000, and if gold continues abundant it may become one of the most important cities on the Pacific coast. San Diego harbour also affords secure anchorage for merchant vessels and runs a considerable distance inland.

Population

The Indian inhabitants have been much diminished by small-pox and 'fire-water'. In 1842 they were numbered at 14,500. It is probable that the number of whites is now 15,000. The Mormons have formed several stations and adventurers are flocking to California from all parts.

Commerce and Industry

Although the auriferous appearance of the soil was first noted by Drake in the sixteenth century, large-scale wet and dry digging for gold has only begun in the last few years. To what extent gold will continue to be found it is impossible to say; some ravines 100 yards long by 4 wide have yielded 17,000 dollars. Other metals also abound, including cinnabar, copper, iron and silver.

The Illustrations by H. Warren & Engraved by R. Wallis.

SCALE

The Map Drawn & Engraved by J. Rapkin.

British America

Area and Physical Aspect

The British dominions in North America comprise an area of nearly 4,000,000 square miles and are divided into nine provinces: East and West Canada, New Brunswick, Nova Scotia, Cape Breton Isle, Prince Edward Isle, Newfoundland, Hudson's Bay Territories and Vancouver's Island. A country of mountain ranges, magnificent rivers, immense lakes, boundless forests, extensive prairies and foaming cataracts, Canada offers the most picturesque natural beauties. Geological evidence suggests that the whole country emerged comparatively recently from the ocean, and that instead of a continent of North America, there was only a succession of islands and rocks.

History

After John Cabot first entered the Gulf of St Lawrence in 1497 the English made no permanent efforts at colonization, and the region was seized in 1541 by the French, who established themselves in what is now East and West Canada. Further north, while searching for the north-west passage in 1517, Sebastian Cabot first penetrated Hudson's Bay but without discovering it to be an enclosed sea. Fretum Hudson sailed through the strait in 1610 and the bay was named after him. Another great bay was named after Baffin, who first traced its outlines. In 1759 the combined British and New England forces under General Wolfe captured Quebec and drove the French out. The present government consists of a House of Assembly, consisting of 84 members chosen by electors possessing a very low qualification, an Executive Council, also elected by the people, and a Legislative Council, nominated by the crown for life. The British monarch is represented by the governor-general.

Revenue

At the time of the British conquest the public income was very trifling. This has now been increased considerably by taxes on imports (£450,000), licensing of inns, ale-houses, auctioneers, steam-boats, hawkers and billiard-tables (£30,000) and tolls on roads, canals, bridges and harbours (£50,000). However, the national debt remains high, with East and West Canada alone owing £327,646 in currency and £869,650 in sterling. At the period of reunion of the provinces in 1840 the British government guaranteed a loan of one and a half million pounds for Canada to be employed in public works, particularly in East and West Canada; and these are now yielding a substantial revenue.

Population

The total number of inhabitants in British America is around 2,335,000, of whom nine-tenths live in the east of the country. Most whites are descended from earlier English and French settlers or have emigrated from England, Scotland, Ireland and the United States. Many religious groups are represented among the people, although most belong either to the Roman Catholic church or to the churches of England and Scotland. Given the vastness of the country, it is sparsely populated and the chief urban centres are concentrated in the regions immediately bordering the St Lawrence and the great lakes. The Hudson's Bay Territories, with an area of three million square miles, has only 200,000 people. It is certain that the country could support many more people than it does at present.

WEST CANADA
VICTORIA DEI GRATIA BRITANNIAR REG F.D. SIGILL PROV CANADAE SUPERIORIS
KINGSTON
FALLS OF NIAGARA
LAKE HURON
GEORGIAN BAY
GREAT MANITOULIN I.
LAKE ONTARIO
LAKE ERIE
MICHIGAN
GRATIOTS BAY
Lake St. Clair
Nottawasaga Bay
Indian Territory
OTTAWA COUNTY
Prince Edward I.
Toronto
Kingston
Hamilton
Goderich
Detroit
Buffaloe
Erie
Erie Canal
Oneida Lake
Sackets Harbour
Montreal
River St. Lawrence
Ottawa or Grand River
SCALE
Longitude West from Greenwich
The Illustrations by H. Warren, & Engraved by Robt. Wallis.
The Map Drawn & Engraved by J. Rapkin.

West Canada

First settled for the most part by refugee loyalists from the United States and emigrants from Britain, West Canada covers an area of 258,000 square miles stretching alongside the St Lawrence river and the great lakes of Ontario, Erie and Huron. The falls of Niagara, by which Lake Erie empties its waters into Lake Ontario, form one of the finest sights in the world. Less populous than neighbouring East Canada, the province has nevertheless seen a tenfold increase in the number of inhabitants in the last 50 years to the present figure of 750,000. Chiefly agricultural, with 2,600,000 acres under cultivation, West Canada had, at the last count two years ago, 565,645 neat cattle and 833,807 sheep. The chief town and seat of Her Majesty's government is Toronto (population 25,000), a flourishing and well-built city near the north-west extremity of Lake Ontario, but there are several other thriving towns, including Kingston, London, Hamilton, Guelph, etc. The Canada Company have a fine tract of about 1 million acres near Lake Huron where they have established several settlements and done much good.

The Hudson's Bay territories of British America extend from the Pacific in the west to Labrador on the Atlantic coast, and have been calculated at 3,060,000 square miles in area. The Hudson's Bay Company was granted a charter by Charles II which gave it trading rights to all those lands within the Hudson's Strait which were not already owned by other persons or nations. At the present time the company controls hunting, trapping and shipping over a vast area and has forts or stockades from Pacific to Atlantic, and from the Arctic Ocean to the Canadian borders. Labrador on the east has been little explored and is, as far as we know, formed of rocks, lakes, swamps and mountains. In the west the Rocky Mountains run almost parallel with the coast right up to the Arctic Ocean. Between the mountains and Hudson's Bay the land is intersected with lakes, marshes and rivers to such an extent that it would seem the inner springs of the earth there burst forth. Some parts are truly desolate. Vegetation ceases in the latitude of 60° N. Further south, in the regions of the Red and Assiniboine rivers the soil is fertile and the climate salubrious; an extensive settlement with stone buildings has been formed there.

The North-Western Archipelago north of Vancouver Island belongs partly to England and partly to Russia. It has several good harbours, though little or nothing is known of the interior of these islands. Queen Charlotte's Island is admirably suited to the formation of a penal settlement, being impossible to escape from and an important position in which the convicts might build a fortress.

When discovered Canada was densely populated by several Indian nations who are now almost extinct, there being only about 35,000 in the whole country. Many of the remaining tribes of Sarcees, Crees, Blackfeet, etc. are in constant war with one another, and are very reluctant to settle and cultivate the land.

EAST CANADA, AND NEW BRUNSWICK.
QUEBEC.
NORTH AMERICAN INDIANS.
SCALE.
Longitude West from Greenwich.
GULF OF ST LAWRENCE
CHALEURS BAY
BAY OF FUNDY
NEW BRUNSWICK
THREE RIVERS
MONTREAL
SHERBROOKE
VICTORIA DEI GRATIA BRITANNIAR. REG. F.D.
SIGILL. PROV. CANADAE. INFERIORIS.
The Illustrations by H. Warren & Engraved by J. B. Allen.
The Map Drawn & Engraved by J. Rapkin.

East Canada and New Brunswick

Originally part of the French Acadia, New Brunswick was colonized by British settlers after the conquest of Quebec in 1761. It contains much variety of scenery in its 26,000 square miles and is marked by several dis tinguishing features. The hills, though none of considerable height, are nevertheless precipitous and sharply defined, giving them an alpine character. The greater part of New Brunswick is still uncultivated though beautiful, containing an abundance of timber and extensive prairies. The chief river, the St John, flows into the Bay of Fundy and is navigable for vessels of 50 tons as far upstream as Fredericton, the capital, 85 miles inland. The city of St John at the mouth of the river is favourably situated for trade and has many wharfs, docks and warehouses.

East Canada is 120,000 square miles in area and has 768,000 inhabitants, making it the most densely populated province in British America. The number of people is rising rapidly and has almost doubled in the last 25 years. The territory was chiefly occupied by the early French settlers and their descendants who established themselves at Quebec and Montreal and still form the majority of the population. There are several thriving towns, including those established by the British American Land Company at Sherbooke and Stanstead in the most fertile part of the province. The chief towns, however, are Quebec and Montreal. Quebec (population 40,000), which was captured by the British in 1759, stands on an eminence 350 feet above the St Lawrence and is the strongest fortress on the whole American continent. Montreal (population 50,000), is a handsome commercial city. These two towns are the seaports of Canada, for the great St Lawrence river which connects them to the Atlantic is navigable for ships of a large class for nearly 2,000 miles. It discharges 4,277,880 million tons of fresh water into the sea every year, of which almost half may be reckoned melted snow. A large part of the country along the banks of the St Lawrence was granted to settlers by the French crown under the system of feudal tenures which still survives in Canada although not in France. Over 10,800,000 acres in the territory are divided into 168 seignories, with 2,500,000 remaining ungranted and surveyed. There is a large inland trade between Canada and the United States, although the Canadians complain, with justice, that their produce is heavily taxed on entering the United States while they receive American goods on favourable terms. The total value of imports to East Canada alone is about £2,500,000 a year. The province is defended by a considerable militia of 36 regiments, consisting of 137,769 men. The principal military stations are at Quebec and Montreal.

To the far west of British America lies the fine island of Vancouver, a land of rich soil, valuable coal seams and excellent anchorage. Well situated as a trading port with the Pacific islands and East Asia, it has recently been granted to the Hudson's Bay Company.

NOVA SCOTIA AND NEWFOUNDLAND
SCALE
NOVA SCOTIA AND CAPE BRETON
NEWFOUNDLAND
LABRADOR
MINGAN DISTRICT
NORTHUMBERLAND
RIVER ST LAWRENCE
CANADIAN CHANNEL
ANTICOSTI ISLD
CANADA EAST
GULF OF ST LAWRENCE
CHALEUR BAY
NEW BRUNSWICK
MAGDALEN Is
PRINCE EDWARD Id
NEWFOUNDLAND
BAY OF ISLANDS
BAY OF ST GEORGE
BAY OF NOTRE DAME
BONAVISTA BAY
TRINITY BAY & DISTT
CONCEPTION BAY & DISTT
FORTUNE BAY
PLACENTIA BAY
St MARYS BAY
FERRYLAND DISTT
CAPE BRETON ISLAND
NOVA SCOTIA
BAY OF FUNDY
Sable I.
ATLANTIC OCEAN
HALIFAX, NOVA SCOTIA
COD FISHERY OFF NEWFOUNDLAND
Longitude West from Greenwich

Nova Scotia and Newfoundland

An extensive peninsula connected with the continent of north America by an isthmus only eight miles wide, Nova Scotia has an area of over 3,000 square miles. The number of rivers and lakes means that there is no point in the province 30 miles from navigable water. Chief of the rivers are the Shubenacadie, at whose mouth the rise and fall of the tide is about 50 feet, and the Annapolis, which is navigable for large vessels for 40 miles above Digby. In number, capacity and security the harbours of Novia Scotia are unsurpassed by those of any other country of similar extent. There are valuable coal mines here and on Cape Breton Island; in 1848 130,779 chaldrons of coal were raised here. Nova Scotia was probably discovered by the Cabots and thereafter ownership of the territory was disputed by English and French until 1736, since when it has been in British ownership. The capital is at Halifax.

Cape Breton Island is separated from Nova Scotia by a narrow channel called the Gut of Canso, which in one place is only one mile broad The island is divided by the great inlet of the sea termed Bras d'Or into two contrasting parts, that on the north being steep, rocky and forbidding, that on the south low and undulating inland but rising to abrupt cliffs near the ocean. Sydney, the capital, is beautifully situated at the head of a fine bay with a secure and capacious harbour.

Prince Edward Island in the gulf of St Lawrence was once covered with forests of birch, beech, maple, spruce, fir, hemlock and cedar to the very edge of the water; the labours of the lumbermen, the progress of cultivation and many destructive fires have greatly thinned their rich luxuriance. The constant action of the tidal waters has indented the island with many creeks and inlets. Of the numerous harbours, the principal is the capital, Charlotte town (population 6,000).

Newfoundland is the nearest to Europe of any part of America and measures 419 by 300 miles at its longest and widest. The oldest of England's colonies, British government was established here in 1583. It stands on two immense banks about 600 miles in length varying in depth from 25 to 150 fathoms. The coast is much indented and the British settlements are almost entirely confined to the shores. The capital, St John, is strongly protected, both by its natural position and by fortifications. The resident population is estimated near 96,000, but the numbers necessarily fluctuate because of the extensive fisheries carried out along the coast. The banks swarm with almost every variety of fish, and much is caught and sold for export. Chief is the cod, although salmon fishing is followed by several families in the summer, the dogfish is caught for its oil and the herring industry is increasing. The total value of fish, oil and skins exported in 1848 was £818,305. In addition 1½ to 2 quintals per month is consumed by each member of the population.

The Illustrations by H. Winkles & Engraved by G.R. Manwaring.

The Map, Drawn & Engraved by J. Rapkin.

Central America

The five states of Guatemala (population 600,000), Salvador (280,000), Honduras (236,000), Nicaragua (226,000) and Costa Rica (95,000) were once united in the federal republic of Central America which was governed by a central congress, senate and president; but in 1839 each state declared itself independent and there is no longer a national government unifying them. The most important of the five is Guatemala.

Area and Physical Aspect

Very mountainous, Guatemala has several active volcanoes of great elevation. The Volcan de Agua has a crater more than 100 yards deep and an upper circumference of 800 yards; while the nearby Volcan de Fuego has never been ascended, owing to the quantity of hot and loose ashes that cover the upper part. The country is watered by three main rivers, the Motagua, the Polochic and the Lacantun, all flowing into the Gulf of Mexico. There are also four extensive lakes, the largest being the Gulf of Dulce which communicates with the Atlantic and could be dredged to admit vessels of 200 to 300 tons

Chief Cities

New Guatemala, the capital (population 40,000), was built in 1776 after Antigua Guatemala had been devastated by an earthquake three years before. It is laid out in quadrilateral form with a great square, 150 yards wide, occupying the centre. Some of the public buildings and churches are massive in construction, but the private houses are only one storey high, to guard against the ill effects of earthquake. Every division of the city is supplied with excellent water, brought from some distance by two aqueducts. Despite its destruction, about 3,000 people still live in the enormous wreck of ruins which is all that remains of the old capital. Next in rank is Quesaltenango (population 20,000), whose great church is 250 feet high and much adorned with sculpture. About 6 leagues from the town of Yzabel there are some singular architectural antiquities of unknown date in the form of columns, ovals and sculpture, which are evidently the production of an ingenious and superior race.

Population

Most of the inhabitants are Indians of different tribes, with a few whites and the remainder Mestizoes and Mulattoes, or a mixed breed of various shades of colour. Chiefly Roman Catholic in religion. For administrative purposes, the country is divided into seven departments, each with its own corregidor. Guatemala has been afflicted by intestine discord and revolutionary proceedings caused by ambitious men seeking power, and the state has also recently been at war with neighbouring San Salvador.

Commerce and Industry

The fertile lands along the Pacific coast serve as pasturage for extensive herds of sheep and cattle. Cacao, cotton, sugar, grains and tobacco are also produced, and the cochineal dye is of such excellent quality that exports have risen markedly in the last 20 years. In 1849 a 'treaty of friendship, commerce and navigation' was concluded between the government of Guatemala and the queen of England which places their produce, when imported, on the same footing as the most favoured nation.

The Illustrations by H. Warren, & Engraved by J. Wrightson.

The Map Drawn & Engraved by J. Rapkin.

The Isthmus of Panama

Since the days of Columbus and Cortez, the great project of connecting the Atlantic with the Pacific by a navigable communication, or at least of facilitating the transit of passengers and merchandise across the Isthmus of Panama (a direct distance of 34 miles at its narrowest) has from time to time engaged the attention of the European and American public. The discovery of gold in California, the personal transit of about 80,000 a year going to the mines for five months and then returning home, and the extraordinary augmentation of California in population and wealth have facilitated the solution of this most important problem.

Humboldt, the great authority on South American affairs, has suggested a number of possible routes, many of them using existing rivers. One proposal for a ship canal is to use Lake Nicaragua, 15 miles from the Pacific coast, and the San Juan River which flow into the Atlantic and has no cataracts, only rapids. Another available route is that between Panama and Porto Bello, where the siting of the Rio Grande, flowing into the Pacific, and the Chagre River, flowing into the Atlantic, would necessitate a canal of only 30 miles to connect them, with a few locks to allow for the difference in tide of about 16 feet between Atlantic and Pacific. In 1788 a parish priest of the country induced his Indian flock to cut a shallow canal between branches of the Quito and San Juan rivers, by which in the rainy season canoes pass from Atlantic to Pacific, a distance of 250 miles.

Two projects undertaken by citizens of the United States are presently in the course of construction. The first is a railroad to go from Panama to Gorgona in the first instance (with a later extension all the way to the Atlantic). Messrs. Howland and Aspinwall of New York have been granted exclusive privilege of transit for 49 years by the republic of New Granada, in addition to harbour rights, title to 300,000 acres for the purposes of colonization and the use of three companies of sappers from New Granada. It is estimated that when complete the railroad will have cost £1,000,000.

The second is a ship canal, via Lake Nicaragua and the San Juan River. A contract for this undertaking was entered into in 1849, between the Republic of Nicaragua and the Atlantic and Pacific Ship Canal Company of New York, who have agreed to complete the work within 12 years. There is some argument with the British government, who refuse to acknowledge Nicaragua's authority to grant rights to the San Juan River, the Mosquito kingdom which touches the river being under the protection of the queen of England; but the cabinets in London and Washington are considering the matter. The estimated cost of the entire canal is £4,000,000.

Finally, Captain Liot of the Royal Mail Steam Packet Company has prepared a detailed report on the advisability of constructing a good macadamized carriage road from Porto Bello to Panama, both towns providing secure anchorage.

The Illustrations by J. Marchant & Engraved by J. Rogers.

The Map Drawn & Engraved by J. Rapkin.

South America

Area and Physical Aspect

The southern portion of the American continent is marked by two striking features: the whole west coast forms a plateau averaging 10,000 feet in height which rises into the Andes mountains; while to the east lies an expanse of level country intersected by three great rivers, the Amazon, La Plata and Orinoco. The length of the continent is about 4,600 miles from north to south, and 3,200 miles from east to west at its widest.

Mountains and Plains

Running along the entire west coast from Panama to the Straits of Magellan, the immense rampart of the Andes narrows towards the southern extremity, becomes suddenly broader to the north of Chili and at Popayan divides into several lesser chains. The vast mountains are granite-based with superincumbent gneiss, mica, slate, greenstone and porphyry. The depth of some of the fissures considerably facilitates geological inquiry. Gold, silver, quicksilver and other metals abound. There are several active volcanoes even amidst the regions of perpetual snow. The immense savannahs or Llanos in the east are so flat and solitary that
Humboldt has likened them to a tranquil ocean covered with sea weeds. There are few human inhabitants, but numerous herds of wild horses and oxen which multiply with great rapidity.

Rivers

The most important river is the Amazon, with a length of about 5,000 miles including its windings. The main trunk is composed of three rivers, the Apurimac, Beni and Tunguragua, but many of the streams descending the eastern Andes swell its waters. The mouth is wide enough to contain an island, Joannes, 175 miles long and 125 broad; and the waters are impelled with such velocity that fresh water is carried 40 leagues into the sea. The La Plata is formed by the Paraguay, Parana and Uruguay. It is navigable for 1,000 miles. The Orinoco combines most of the rivers that water the Caracas and the eastern part of New Granada, draining an area of 400,000 square miles. During the inundations from April to October a large area of the delta is under water.

Vegetable and Animal Kingdom

The gradations of plants and trees are naturally regulated by differences of latitude and elevation. Alpine plants appear in a zone of 6,000 to 12,600 feet, while grasses grow even higher, carpeting the mountains with gold. At the southern extremity and on the highest peaks vegetation almost ceases. The vast tropical forests along the river margins in the east abound with strange and beautiful orchids and parasitic plants, while lilies and other aquatic plants are of a size unknown to Europe. Unmolested by man, the forest animals range from jaguar to brightly coloured beetles, tapir to boa-constrictor. That singular fish, the electric eel, is found only in South America.

Population

When discovered by the Spaniards at the close of the fifteenth century South America was densely peopled and had many large cities; but the ruthless policy of the conquerors and the vices and diseases they introduced destroyed millions of the Indians.

VENEZUELA, NEW GRANADA, EQUADOR, AND THE GUAYANAS
CARIBBEAN SEA
CHIMBORAZO
FALL OF THE BAGOTA
PARAMARIBO
BRAZIL
PERU
ECUADOR
NEW GRANADA
VENEZUELA
BRITISH GUAYANA
DUTCH GUAYANA
FRENCH GUAYANA
COSTA RICA
GULF OF DARIEN
BAY OF PANAMA
GULF OF VENEZUELA
Gulf of Guayaquil
SCALE
Equator
Dominica
Martinique
St. Lucia
Barbadoes
S. Vincent
Grenadines
Granada
Tobago
Trinidad
Caracas
Panama
Quito
Guayaquil
Cuenca
Angostura
Sierra Pacaraima
R. Negro
R. Maranon or Amazons

Venezuela, New Granada, Equador and The Guayanas

When they first attained independence from Spain in 1819, these three states were formed into a confederation known as the Republic of Columbia; but on the death of Simon Bolivar in 1830, three separate republics were formed, each with their own elected president. There are frequent internal revolutions.

VENEZUELA

Traversed from west to east by the Orinoco river, the country is bounded by a cordillera of mountains which give rise to the extraordinary magnificence of the scenery. The coast has numerous gulfs and bays, the largest the Gulf of Venezuela which communicates with the lake of Maracaibo, a vast inland sea. The climate is intensely hot and moist in the valleys, cool on the mountains, and no country is more frequently visited by earthquakes. Caracas, the capital, is picturesquely situated at the foot of the Silla mountains. The chief commerce is in live stock, with cattle rearing on the savannahs of the Orinoco being the principal branch of business, though cacao, coffee, tobacco and sugar are also cultivated and exported in large quantities. The total population numbers about 1,267,000, including whites, Indians, Mestigos and slaves.

NEW GRANADA

The leading feature of this country is the northern part of the great Andes chain. On an extensive table-land 7,000 feet above the sea, the capital, Santa Fe de Bogota, stands encircled by mountains. The majestic Magdalena River crosses the land from north to south, and other rivers have been extended by canals built by the Indians to provide a means of inland navigation from the Atlantic to the Pacific. Numerous rivers with short courses also descend from the west face of the Andes, falling in striking cataracts up to 650 feet high down almost perpendicular rock. On the banks of all the rivers the soil is extremely fertile, and many different kinds of tree grow there, including oak, ebony and mahogany. The area also produces many dye stuffs and drugs, including balsam, cochineal, sarsaparilla, liquorice, cassia and quinquina, or Jesuit's bark. Silver ore and precious stones are found in several places. The chief towns include Cartagena and Santa Martha on the north coast, and Buenaventura on the Pacific coast. At the last count, in 1835, the population numbered 1,686,038.

EQUADOR

This republic (population about 600,000) contains some of the highest peaks in the Andes, among them Chimborazo, 21,440 feet, and Cotopaxi. This last is an active volcano of nearly 19,000 feet, which has had several major eruptions in the eighteenth century, including one which sent flames 3,000 feet above the brink of the crater; and it continues to eject prodigious quantities of mud. Several villages are at a height of 13,000 feet above the sea, and the remains can be seen of an extraordinary road built by the Incas which Humboldt considers the equal of the finest Roman roads in Italy and France. The principal port is Guayaquil, one of the handsomest towns in South America, which has a population of about 10,000.

PERU & BOLIVIA
SWIMMING COURIERS OF PERU
TARIJA
POTOSI
LIMA
ECUADOR
BRAZIL
PERU
BOLIVIA
LA PLATA
MOXOS
CHIQUITOS
ATACAMA
SCALE
Miles
Longitude West 70 from Greenwich
C. S. Lorenzo
Guayaquil
Gulf of Guayaquil
Tumbez
Truxillo
Caxamarca
Moyobamba
Huaura
P. of Callao
Lima
Tarma
Jauja
Huanta
Huanca velica
Cuzco
Puno
Arequipa
Arica
Port Iquique
Cobija
Atacama Alta
Coquimbo
Apolobamba
La Paz
Oruro
Potosi
Chuquisaca
Tarija
Cochabamba
Exaltacion
Concepcion
Matto Grosso
S. Xavier
Santiago
Nova Coimbra
Fᵗ Principe de Beira
R. Maranon or Amazons
R. Purus
R. Madeira
R. Paraguay
R. Parana
R. Vermejo
R. Ucayali
Tabatinga
Olivenca
Pauxis or Obydos
L. Titicaca

Peru and Bolivia

Area and Physical Aspect

The republic of Peru has an area of about 300,000 square miles traversed by the Andes and six other chains of mountains. The highest summit in the region is the dome of Chuquibamba, at 22,000 feet, and there are several other volcanic cones of great altitude. Chief among the many lakes is Titicaca, which is fed by ten rivers and dotted with islands. There are four climates in Peru: that of the coast, which is dry and temperate; that of the sierras, mild and variable; that of the Andes, piercingly cold, and that of the pampas, warm and humid. The sierras are said to be the most healthy place in the world; in 1765 a Spaniard living there died at the age of 144, leaving 800 lineal descendants.

History

When the Spaniards arrived in 1526-7, the Peruvian empire had been flourishing for 400 years under twelve Incas or sovereigns. The European conquerors were interested solely in the acquisition of riches and ruthlessly destroyed the Indians. Indeed there is probably no other part of the world where, within the space of 300 years, so much human blood has been shed. Finally, after a series of struggles the Peruvians gained their independence in 1821 and every European Spaniard was expelled. The present republic is governed by an elected chief.

Chief Cities

Lima, the capital, was founded by Pizarro in 1535 and was for many years the largest and richest city in South America. However, it has suffered severely from earthquakes, with two-thirds of the buildings being destroyed in 1746. The estimated population is 60,000, of whom about one quarter are Creoles and Europeans. Cusco, the ancient capital, contains 20,000 inhabitants, and the Inca palace and temple there have been turned into a Roman Catholic cathedral and a nunnery.

Population

To judge from its great temples, extensive roads and enormous cemeteries, Peru must at one period have possessed numerous inhabitants. The present population is estimated vaguely at 1,700,000 to 2,000,000. Potatoes form the chief ingredient in the food of the people.

Trade and Industry

Agriculture has been much neglected, although the vegetable riches are great and varied. Far more important is the mineral wealth which, despite centuries of exploitation by the Spanish, is still inexhaustible. Gold, silver, copper and lead are all mined in great quantities.

Bolivia or High Peru

Formerly part of Peru, this independent republic (population estimated 1,300,000) was named after the Liberator. Covering an area of 1,480,000 square miles it is mostly mountainous, with some peaks reaching over 24,000 feet. The famed silver mine of Potosi is in a conical shaped mountain 20 miles in circumference and has been worked since 1545; the town of Potosi was once the most populous city in South America. The latest known capital was Chiquisaca. La Paz city, situated in a gulf 12,194 feet above the sea, is a great emporium for merchandise in transit to the interior. We have no details of trade.

The Illustrations by H.Winkles, & Engraved by W.Lacey.

The Map Drawn & Engraved by J. Rapkin.

Chili and La Plata

Chili

This republic, extending along the coast of the Pacific, has an area of about 250,000 square miles. The northern districts were once provinces of the ancient Peruvian empire, conquered by the Spanish; but the further south the Europeans proceeded the more determined they found their foe, and insurrections against Spain continued throughout the centuries until independence was achieved in 1823. Most of the country is made up of a vast plain rising gradually from the ocean to the Andes, whose lofty peaks are as much as 20,000 feet high in places. The whole area is watered and fertilized by innumerable streams or torrents. Santiago, the capital, and Valparaiso, the port of Santiago, are the two largest cities, and there are several fine harbours. The population of about one million live in eleven provinces. Although the country was poor and badly cultivated under Spanish sway, there are now fertile farms, fine villages, schools and public institutions. Rich in minerals, Chili has at least one thousand copper mines and exports great quantities of this metal.

Araucania

This tract of country lying south of Chili proper is very little known. The brave inhabitants have successfully resisted attempts by the Spanish, Chilians or Peruvians to destroy their independence. Valdivia is the chief town, the government is complicated and refined, the people hospitable and the climate salubrious.

Buenos Ayres and La Plata

This region of about 1,000,000 square miles resembles an extensive amphitheatre, surrounded as it is on three sides by mountains. The country is generally level and covered in lakes and rivers, among them the La Plata, which is formed by the junction of the Paraguay, Uruguay and Parana and is navigable for 1,000 miles. The immense plains extending westward from the banks of the Paraguay are called pampas and are inhabited by the guachos and other scattered Indian tribes who, possessed of an abundance of wild horses and horned cattle, roam the country in a state of savage independence. The high road from Buenos Ayres to Santiago lies across these trackless plateaux and is traversed by caravans. Originally one of the United Provinces of Rio de la Plata, which included what are now Uruguay and the Argentine Confederation, Buenos Ayres was founded in 1535 and now has a population of about 500,000. Apart from the native Indians, the people are mostly Creoles and Negroes, with a few European Spaniards. Defective as a commercial port, since there is no harbour and the water is too shallow for large vessels, the city of Buenos Ayres nevertheless acts as a centre for internal and foreign trade, mostly in hides, skin, horn and other animal products. For this reason it is also a centre for intercourse between the local administrations and foreign governments. General Rosas, the governor of Buenos Ayres, has usurped a kind of dictatorial power over the neighbouring states but can exercise no legal jurisdiction over them unless it has been conferred by a general congress.

FALKLAND ISLANDS AND PATAGONIA
JASON ISLANDS
PENGUINS
SEA EAGLES
FUEGEANS
CHRISTMAS SOUND. TIERRA DEL FUEGO.
WEST FALKLAND
EAST FALKLAND
FALKLAND SOUND
GULF OF SAN MATIAS
GULF OF ST GEORGE
PATAGONIA
TIERRA DEL FUEGO
STRAIT OF MAGALHAENS
SCALE

Falkland Islands and Patagonia

FALKLAND ISLANDS

Called Malouine by the French and Maluinas by the Spanish, this group of islands was discovered by an Englishman, Captain David, in 1592. After that time they were virtually ignored for nearly a century, despite the recognition of their value as a refreshment place for ships doubling Cape Horn; but during the eighteenth century both the French and the Spanish made attempts to occupy the islands and they were finally declared a colony of her Britannic Majesty in 1842. There are two principal islands, West and East Falkland, with a considerable number of smaller islands clustered around them, altogether covering a surface of about 6,000 square miles. The lower lands appear to consist of clay-slate, while the higher rugged hills, rising on some islands to more than 2,000 feet, are of quartz. A peculiar geological feature are the streams of stones which appear to be flowing down the sides of the hills. Deeply indented by sounds, creeks and harbours, the coastline is among the most irregular in the world. East Falkland is the best known at present and contains the government settlement at Port William. The population is still very scanty, although wild cattle abound and vessels can obtain very cheap beef (2*d*. per lb.). The climate is healthy and more equable than in England, with little ice or snow. The soil is dark and peaty. There are no trees but a few stunted evergreens.

PATAGONIA

This extensive region of about 135,000,000 acres was named by its discoverer, Magellan. Only the maritime part has been explored and that but partially, although the country has considerable value as a point of communication with Chili and Peru and for extending trade from the Atlantic to the Pacific. A large part of the country belongs to Great Britain. In addition to the mountains of the Andean chain, Patagonia has several active volcanoes. Judging from the herds of wild horses, oxen, deer, guanacoes and game of all sorts, there must be abundance of good land; the many rivers flow mostly in a south-easterly direction from the mountains and are full of fish. The population is very small; some say only a few thousand, living in distinct nomadic tribes. Tall in nature and of enormous strength, the people live to a great age, many to over 100 years. For such a high southern latitude the climate is peculiarly mild, the atmosphere very salubrious.

TIERRA DEL FUEGO

This island, 42,000 square miles in area in separated from Patagonia by narrow straits, in some places only 3 miles wide. In 1582 the King of Spain attempted to set up a colony here to control the passage into the pacific, but famine and cold compelled the abandonment of this design.

CAPE HORN

The southernmost point of Admiral Hermites's Islands, Cape Horn has long presented a fearful challenge to navigators. For many centuries all this group of islands were supposed to belong to a great south land which stretched along the Polar region to include New Zealand.

BRAZIL
BOATS ON THE RIO NEGRO.
St CATHARINA.
MONTE VIDEO.
CAPE St ANTONIO, BAHIA.
RIO DE JANEIRO.
NORTH ATLANTIC OCEAN
SOUTH ATLANTIC OCEAN
Equator
GUAYANA
VENEZUELA
BOLIVIA
LA PLATA
SOLIMOES
URUGUAY
S. PAULO
Trinidad
Georgetown
Paramaribo
Cayenne
Rio Maranon or Amazons
Rio Para
Maranhao
Natal
C. St Roque
Parahyba
Recife
Cuyaba
Matto Grosso
Asuncion
Victoria
ESPIRITU SANTO
RIO DE JANEIRO
S.SALVADOR or Bahia
B. de Todos Santos
Porto Seguero
R.S.Francisco
I.S.Catharina
Rio Grande
BUENOS AYRES
Monte Video
Rio de la Plata
SCALE.
Longitude West from Greenwich

Brazil, Uruguay and Paraguay

Brazil

This country, so-called from *braza*, a valuable indigenous wood, comprehends almost a third part of the South American continent. It has a maritime boundary stretching from the Oyapoke River in the north to the Chuy in the south, a distance of some 2,620 miles. Estimated at 3,000,000 square miles in area, the country consists mainly of wooded plains and vast forests, with the highest mountain chain running more than 1,400 miles more or less parallel with the coast and reaching 6,000 feet. Many ridges remain uninvestigated and the centre of the country is almost an unknown land, except to the dwellers in it. Of its almost innumerable rivers, the chief is the mighty Maranon or Amazon, which flows through 1,600 miles of Brazilian territory. First occupied by the Portuguese in 1504, the country was used as a penal settlement for 50 years or so, then thrown open for colonization. The Dutch, French, Spanish and English have all tried at various times to invade but have been expelled. The colony claimed independence from Portugal in 1822 and Brazil is now the only royal government in America with its own emperor and legislative assembly. The chief city is Rio de Janeiro which is built on one of the finest harbours in the world with an interior bay 100 miles in compass. From the harbour the city appears rich and magnificent, but the streets are narrow and the architecture of many private dwellings is poor. The total population in 1825 was over five million (excluding the Indian tribes) of whom about one million are white, the remainder African slaves, free blacks and Creoles. The chief products are sugar, coffee, cotton, various medicines, Indian rubber, timber of all kinds, gold and diamonds. Trade is conducted mainly with Great Britain, the United States and Portugal.

Uruguay

After a long struggle between Brazil and Buenos Ayres, this territory was made a republic in 1828. It has an area of 10,500 squares miles and a population of about 250,000, chiefly of Spanish descent although many foreigners are now being naturalized. The capital, Monte Video, lies on the Plate River which forms the southern boundary. This city derives its name from the good look-out obtained by its position on a promontory. Admirably adapted for the rearing of cattle and farming on a large scale, the country has a constitution which gives great facilities for naturalization and encourages the immigration of Europeans.

Paraguay

This province declared itself an independent republic in 1810. With a surface area of about, 30,000 square miles it lies to the south-west of Brazil. The chief city Asuncion is situated on the Paraguay River which forms the whole of its western boundary. We know nothing of the interior. The Great Chaco, an immense tract inhabited by Indians, is in part claimed by and nominally under the government of Paraguay, but in reality unexplored. The total population has been variously estimated from 800,000 to 1,000,000.

BRITISH GUAYANA
ATLANTIC OCEAN
GEORGETOWN
NEW AMSTERDAM
CHRISTMAS CATARACT, RIVER BERBICE
ATARAIPU
OR THE DEVIL'S ROCK
DUTCH GUAYANA
VENEZUELA
R. Orinoco
Imataca
Pt. Parima or Sabaneta
Sierra Imataca
R. Essequibo
R. Demerara
Georgetown
R. Berbice
New Amsterdam
R. Corentyn
R. Cuyuni
R. Mazaruni
R. Rupununi
R. Branco or Parima
Ft. S. Joaquim
Pacaraima Mts.
Macusis
Wapishanas
Atorais
Carawaimi Mts.
Tarumas
Woyawais
Sierra Acarai
Dense Forest
Dutch Guayana
SCALE
10 20 30 40 50 60 Miles
Longitude West from Greenwich

British Guayana

Area and Physical Aspect

This valuable part of our dominions extends about 200 miles along that portion of South America known as the 'Main' and comprises the settlements on the rivers Essequibo, Demerara and Berbice. Altogether it covers an area of nearly 100,000 square miles. The limits have never yet been completely settled and the exact inland boundaries are therefore unclear. With the exception of ranges of sandstone hills extending 20 to 30 miles inland the part inhabited by Europeans is flat and alluvial, and drained by canals and sluices. Around 100 miles inland there are fine savannahs interrupted by hill and dale country and high rocky land. The three great rivers already named are fed by numerous tributaries and flow into the Atlantic. They are navigable for some distance upstream and in the Essequibo the tides can be felt 100 miles from the oceaan. The interior of the colony is crossed by numberless small rivers which run through wild and almost impenetrable forests. In the rainy season these empty themselves into the larger rivers in torrents. The whole coastal area from the Maranon to the Orinoco is low and covered with mangrove bushes. The climate is very moist, tropical and insalubrious to Europeans on their early residence in the country.

History

Originally occupied by the Dutch, the colonies on the Essequibo and Demerara passed through English and French hands before being restored to the Dutch in 1802. The following year, however, England again took possession of them and they have belonged to Great Britain since. During their periods of ownership the Dutch parcelled much of the country out into allotments, constructed fine wooden houses and developed the country to a high pitch of prosperity.

Chief Towns

The capital, George Town, on the east bank of the Demerara, might be mistaken for a Dutch city, were it not for the tropical foliage around it. The houses are raised on supports to prevent damps, and many are provided with their own cisterns for the preservation of rain water. The barracks, hospitals and public buildings are in evidence of the taste and munificence of the colonists at whose cost they have been erected. Near the mouth of the Berbice stands New Amsterdam, also intersected by canals, which has all the advantage of the tides.

Population

There are about 125,000 inhabitants, white and coloured. Many emancipated Negroes have acquired no inconsiderable wealth, and in several instances they have purchased estates on which they formerly worked as slaves. There has been great depreciation in some of the landed property in Guyana, but the colonists have spent nearly one million dollars on the importation of Coolies from the East Indies to work as labourers in the plantations.

Commerce and Industry

The staple products are sugar, rum and coffee, to which it is hoped cotton may soon be added. Many estates have their own sugar-mills driven by wind or steam, and being situated by the banks of rivers they have also built their own wharves or landing-places for the convenience of shipping produce.

WEST INDIA ISLANDS.
SEAL OF JAMAICA.
KINGSTON, JAMAICA, FROM THE COMMERCIAL ROOMS.
NORTH ATLANTIC OCEAN
GULF OF MEXICO
BAHAMA ISLANDS
CARIBBEE ISLANDS
LEEWARD
WINDWARD ISLANDS
CARIBEEAN SEA
COLOMBIA
FLORIDA
ST DOMINGO OR HAYTI
PORTO RICO
KINGSTON & Port Royal
Lake of Maracaybo
TRINIDAD
Barbadoes
Martinique
Dominica
Guadaloupe
Antigua
Barbuda
St Christopher
St Vincent
St Lucia
Grenada
Tobago
Margarita
Curaçao
CARTAGENA
Panama
Chagres
Blewfields
Gr. Cayman
Longitude West from Greenwich
SCALE.

West India Islands

Stretching in the form of an arch between North and South America, these islands are most favourably situated for trade with the vast regions around them; and in the event of the Isthmus of Panama becoming a highway between the Atlantic and Pacific, they will be in direct track between Europe and Asia. There are four main groups of islands: the Greater Antilles, of which Jamaica is British, Cuba and Porto Rico are Spanish and Hayti is independent; the Bahamas which are British; the Caribee, which are divided into Leeward and Windward; and the Lesser Antilles, along the coast of South America (both these two groups consisting of islands belonging to various European powers). Like volcanic islands generally, mostly elevated and rugged, the West Indies abound with fine havens and thick swampy forests. The cultivation of cane has given a civilized appearance to many of the islands, while towns built by English, French and Spanish colonists are magnificent in scale.

Principal Islands

Cuba, the largest, is divided into two by a chain of mountains extending from east to west. Havanna, the capital, has one of the finest harbours in the world. Taken by the British in 1762, it was later restored to the Spanish in exchange for the Floridas. Jamaica, also with a range of lofty mountains traversing the island, has its capital in Spanish Town. Hayti has a central range of mountains and extensive fertile plains. The very beautiful island of Trinidad contains a remarkable pitch lake and several craters. Guadalupe has an active volcano of 5,500 feet.

History

The first land seen by Columbus on his voyage of 1492 was one of the Bahamas, which he gratefully named San Salvador, and on subsequent voyages he saw nearly all the islands in the group, calling them West Indies because he thought he had reached the islands off the coast of India. During the seventeenth century the islands were infested by pirates whose efforts were directed chiefly against the Spanish. Although granted to the monarch of Spain by the Pope, various islands were occupied by other European powers, including the English, French, Danes, Dutch, and Swedes. The original inhabitants were killed in their millions by the avarice and cruelty of the early European settlers, who massacred and enslaved them. After 1503 the nefarious trade in African slaves began, and continued over two centuries, with 30,000,000 Negroes being imported. In 1834 slavery was abolished throughout the British Empire, the slave-owners in the colonies being granted the enormous sum of £20,000,000 as compensation. Slavery still exits, however, in the Spanish and Dutch West Indies. The only independent island, Hayti, is a Negro state of some 1,000,000 inhabitants with an emperor and a representative assembly.

Industry and Commerce

Although sugar has been the chief crop, many of the properties are now depressed and it is hoped that cotton, tobacco, silk, spices and other valuable articles for which the islands are well adapted will be found far more lucrative products and lead to a renewal of prosperity.

JAMAICA
SCALE
Miles
SEAL OF THE COLONY
PORT ROYAL HARBOUR
KINGSTON
PORT ANTONIO
SUGAR MILL
Longitude West from Greenwich
CORNWALL
MIDDLESEX
SURREY
HANOVER
WESTMORELAND
ST ELIZABETH
MANCHESTER
TRELAWNEY
ST ANNE
ST MARY
ST THOMAS IN THE VALE
ST DOROTHY
ST CATHERINE
VERE
CLARENDON
PORTLAND
ST THOMAS IN THE EAST
ST GEORGE
ST ANDREW
PORT ROYAL
ST DAVID
KINGSTON
SPANISH TOWN
Montego Bay
Martha Brea
Port Maria
Port Antonio
Morant Pt.
Portland Pt.
Black River
Savanna la Mar
Mandeville
Old Harbour
N. Negril
S. Negril

Jamaica

AREA AND PHYSICAL ASPECT

This magnificent island, measuring 150 miles long and 55 broad, contains 4,000,000 acres. An elevated ridge, called the Blue Mountains and towering in places to nearly 8,000 feet, runs east to west across the island and is occasionally intersected by other high ridges traversing from north to south. Most of the mountains are conical in form with dark and deep ravines between them denominated 'cockpits'. Upwards of 200 rivers further enhance the island's beauty, though few are navigable for vessels of any burthen. Difficult of access from the south coast, on the north the mountains decline into round-topped hills covered with all the exquisite verdure of the tropics. Jamaica presents every indication of volcanic origin, although there is no volcano in action. The soil is generally deep and fertile and several metals have been found, including lead ore impregnated with silver and fourteen different sorts of rich copper ore. The air is remarkably light and enlivening, producing great cheerfulness even in old age. There are four seasons: vernal rains; hot, dry summers; rainy hurricane months in autumn and cool and serene winters. The medium heat in Kingston throughout the year is 80° F and the minimum 70°, though the temperature naturally decreases as the country is ascended.

HISTORY

Discovered by Christopher Columbus in May 1494 during his second expedition, Jamaica began to be colonized by the Spaniards in 1503. By 1558 the aborigines had entirely perished and slaves were introduced. In 1655 the island was conquered by the English and has remained a British colony since.

CHIEF TOWNS AND HARBOURS

The island is divided into three counties, Middlesex, Surrey and Cornwall, each of which is subdivided into parishes.The seat of government is at Spanish Town (population about 5,000), a town of imposing Spanish buildings in the county of Middlesex, which also contains the splendid King's House, erected and furnished by British colonists at a cost of £50,000. But Kingston, in Surrey, is in reality the capital, and the two towns are joined by the island's only railroad. Situated on a gentle slope, enclosed by a semi-circle of mountains, Kingston overlooks a secure harbour. Lower Kingston is laid out in long straight streets of mathematical regularity. Altogether the island has sixteen principal secure havens, among them Port Antonio and Port Morant, both commodious, and 30 bays, roads or shipping stations which afford good anchorage. The roads throughout the island are in general narrow but good; the making of some roads has cost £700 per mile.

POPULATION

The total number of inhabitants is from 380,000 to 400,000. Yellow fever has occasionally visited the island and committed fearful ravages especially among the white population. Now (December, 1850) cholera is sweeping off large numbers of the coloured inhabitants as well. In several places half the people have been destroyed.

INDUSTRY AND COMMERCE

The staple exports are sugar, rum, coffee and pimento. A valuable copper mine is about to be worked at Annotta Bay, and it is expected that cotton will also be exported soon.